Grace, Faith and Glory

Grace, Faith and Glory
Freedom in Christ

Dominic Smart

Authentic
LIFESTYLE

Copyright © 2003 Dominic Smart

First published in 2003 by Keswick Ministries and Authentic Lifestyle

09 08 07 06 05 04 03   7 6 5 4 3 2 1
Authentic Lifestyle is an imprint of Authentic Media,
PO Box 300, Carlisle, Cumbria, CA3 0QS, UK
and PO Box 1047, Waynesboro, GA 30830-2047
www.paternoster-publishing.com

The right of Dominic Smart to be
identified as the Author of this Work has been
asserted by him in accordance with
Copyright, Designs and Patents Act 1988

British Library Cataloguing in Publication Data

A catalogue record for this book is available from
the British Library

ISBN 1-85078-533-3

Cover design by Ben Hull
Printed in Great Britain by
Cox and Wyman, Reading

Contents

Acknowledgements

As ever, my wife Marjorie and our four children, Meredith, Stephanie, Melissa and Matthew, have borne the brunt of my writing. They have done the most to give me time and space to write, and have put up more than anyone else with my absences, frustrations and deadlines. I love you.

Many others have been a tremendous help. Thank you to those who responded very positively to a short series of pastoral letters on this theme in the Gilcomston Record during 2002. My thanks also the Keswick Convention Committee for inviting me to speak at the 2002 Convention on a particularly relevant passage in Galatians. Preparing for that and being there were a huge blessing to me. The congregation here at Gilcomston have prayed as deadlines have come and gone; by the time you read this all your prayers will have been answered! Special thanks go to Ali Hull for the initial impetus to write this book and for such determined editorial work since.

If this book helps anyone out of the snares and pains of legalism and into a fuller enjoyment of God then I will be glad, and will gladly give the glory to the God who made us all.

Aberdeen, April 2003

What is this book about?

There are, broadly speaking, two ways that the devil will knock a Christian out of the saddle. The first is the way that we're all well aware of – it's the way of wicked flesh, of 'notorious sin'. We give in to temptation, sometimes almost against our will, sometimes with abandon. Rebellious against God's sovereign holiness, we go our own way. Like foolish sheep we wander from the kingly one, who would shepherd us with grace and righteousness, provision and protection. The pages of Scripture are covered with stories, commands, and doctrines to guide us away from sin and closer to God; to sanctify us.

The other way that the devil loves to bring us down occupies more pages of the Bible than we might think. It was a huge problem in the early church. Had it not been, we wouldn't have Galatians and probably wouldn't have Hebrews; we'd also have to take out bits of Acts, Romans, 2 Corinthians, Philippians and Colossians. Jesus faced it and was crucified by its devotees; it was rife throughout most of the years of Israel's history, and it was explicitly not the way for God's people to live as far back as Abraham. There's a strong argument for seeing its opposites spelled out in Eden as well. It is burdensome, lethally plausible and, tragically, it's still rife.

It's legalism, and it really is a sin.

It also needs to be defined clearly here, at the outset. We tend to use the word to refer to an attitude that brings in rules where we don't want them. But legalism isn't a matter of having rules, instructions or limits in our fellowships. As we'll see, it's not the existence of rules that is the problem; it's what we expect those rules to do. Legalism – real legalism, the sort that we find in the Bible and which hamstrings our fellowships – is a way of making and keeping yourself acceptable to God.

Yet so subtle and crafty is the enemy of souls that the problem has been successfully sold to us along the lines of the common use of the word. In our desire to avoid the redefined version we tend to compound our problems, giving the wilful flesh even more license and making our longed-for sanctification recede ever further over the horizon.

This book is about the real problem, the really deadly version of legalism. We are all, in fact, just as familiar with it as we are with 'notorious sin'. It infects us individually, and it infects our churches – of whatever hue they may be. You can suffer under it or make others suffer from your legalism in old-fashioned, conservative, died in the wool, sparsely populated and undecorated little mission halls. You can find it or foster it in the most novel, reactionary, big-buzz manically post-evangelically anti-traditionalist far out charismatic fellowships on this or any other planet. Whatever the style or label of our fellowships, legalism's infection can kill.

This book is written for one reason. If this doesn't sound too strange, it's written for the sheer pleasure and enjoyment of deliverance. When God delivers a Christian from an oppressive burden that has weighed them down for years, it's an especially wonderful experience and brings great glory to God. For such deliverance brings release into the joy of the Lord: his in us and ours in him. That joy, and the glory that God receives in it, are why these pages are written. This book will have done its work if we can find joy in the Lord and in his wonderful grace, joy in that glory of God which is combined by him with the glory of a church redeemed and delivered from the power of sin.

To reach that end we have to be really clear about the real nature of the problem. First, then, a little careful defining has to be done. We have to undo the devil's spin and establish again just what legalism is, diagnosing the disease so that we might be delivered from it by the full range of biblical cures. Then we can go on to look at the problem in closer detail and take in the cures. Among the problems, we will look at legalism's utter uselessness against sin and its futility as a means of bringing us near to God; problems that are answered by the truth about sin and by a larger view of the holiness of God. We'll also see what kind of damage legalism does to the gospel and how we can repair that damage with the truth of the gospel of grace. Finally, we'll expose the greatest problem that legalism brings, that of robbing God of his lordship and glory, to the end that we might live under the perfect freedom of his sovereignty and for the great end of glorifying him.

1

The Real Problem

Two Sufferers

To start from a point that many of us will recognise, I want to describe two fictitious but authentic characters, composed from real people, whose conditions we will encounter throughout the rest of the book. You might identify strands of your own experience in one or both of them.

The girl

Abi was up against it from the beginning.

Her church was a classic den of legalism. Surrounded from her youth by spiritual policemen and judges, she never learned about another way to be a Christian – a way of grace, a way of resting in Christ. All the standards – true, false, good, bad, spiritual, 'worldly' – were set for her by these men. The spoken and unspoken lists of do's and don'ts, with which her Christian life was defined, came from them. From them and through the rest of the fellowship, came the codes that unlocked so-called spiritual progress and assurance. From them came the rungs by which she was supposed to climb to God and find acceptance with him.

Abi didn't know that spiritual chauvinism and biblically ignorant pseudo-piety had robbed her of the innocence of her child-like heart. She had never heard of spiritual abuse and didn't know that it had scarred her emotions and her spirit. She thought that it was normal, this repressive cloud of dominance. She thought that the joyless life was the only holy one and that guilt was what you were saved for as well as from. The gospel as good news had always left her slightly bewildered. What on earth was good about this kind of life? The other girls in the office had more fun and most of them were nicer than her friends (was that really the word?) at church. The wonders of God's love for her and the soaring joys of worship with other believers were alien to her: the unknown language of a foreign and suspect land.

For years she had tried hard and then harder to make the thing work, to be loved and to find the warmth of loving. One summer mission had lifted the clouds and the glow of that bright fellowship had stayed with her into the dankness of autumn. Yet it too had gone. She'd been told later that some of the team had been 'worldly'. She'd thought that too at the time, but she'd noticed that it hadn't seemed to stop them enjoying God and each other. They were even better at witnessing than she was, with their make-up and their new clothes. She'd never felt inferior with them then, just happy. But one November evening after the Bible Study, in the car outside her house, her elder had shown her the real nature of the experience, had guided her into a correct understanding of their faults, had made her feel familiarly dowdy, inside and out. She would never have thought of the word, but after the sincere monologue she went intimidated into the house and into something called sanctity. She felt safe. Safe as a prisoner returned to her cell. Safe from the big bad world outside. She even smiled at the unsmilingly righteous wardens the following Sunday morning.

Safe, until she met Ed at work. Ed, who was witty and courteous but who also enjoyed a beer. Ed, who was doing well and was quiet and polite. Ed who listened as she witnessed and who didn't mind her going to church; he even went along with her. Ed, who took her bowling and then for a take-away, to the cinema and back to his flat. Ed, whose parents were so pleasant and whose parents' house was so tastefully done. Ed, who enjoyed her company and never made points to her but asked her questions about herself. Ed, who kissed her tenderly and not like the clumsy oaf at the youth fellowship. Ed, who took her out on Sunday afternoons and who didn't seem to feel guilty about missing the evening service. Ed, who read novels and listened to jazz and knew about wine. Ed, who opened her up to a world that was forbidden out of fear and ignorance but which seemed just too fascinating and fulfilling to be a flesh-pot. Ed, who made her feel loved; who was very patient about her reluctance to go to bed with him. Ed who proposed and got his 'Yes!' Ed, who unknowingly unlocked her heart and released her from a cage to which she never returned. And Ed, who never understood the void in Abi's heart nor the longing for God with which she silently ached nor the wistful guilt that came and went at Easter nor the sudden, fierce determination to take the children to the local Sunday School. Ed, who never realised that Abi missed the baby and sometimes the bathwater.

The man

He toiled at his Christianity.

Mark's church had been started by folk who were unbearably unhappy with the kind of fellowship that Abi belonged to. Frustrated by the obvious legalism and its formalities, dissatisfied with the restrictive and joyless life that it had produced, they had set up a new church. Not for them the dead hand of legalism.

But that was twenty years ago, fourteen years before Mark had become a Christian and had started going along there with his friends. Now the new patterns had become old ones. The clean slate had become overwritten with many traditions. The church was still seen as very new by the denominational churches around, but it had become set in its ways. Mark loved the music and the style. He loved the informality of the dress-code. He had made good friends there and knew that he owed a great deal to its leaders.

But he toiled, and he didn't know why. He knew that there were people who did things very differently elsewhere and who, despite the warnings from the Pastor, seemed in fact to have the Spirit at work in their churches too. He knew people from supposedly 'dead' churches in a denomination that was reported to have 'Ichabod' written over it, who were relaxed and lively, biblically informed and evangelistically-minded. Why did they seem at ease being a Christian, and why did he seem to have to work hard to belong? Why were his questions about the other Christians never answered? Why was he warned against having coffee with the ex-elder from his own church who had been anathematised and with whose daughter he was good friends? What had that ex-elder done wrong? All he had seemed to do, when Mark boiled it down, was disagree with the Pastor. Why did Mark feel that he was getting a 'look' from the front if he wasn't raising his hands like nearly everyone else did when they sang? Why did he feel that, try as he might, he wasn't really accepted? And why was he made to feel that this was a matter of not being 'where he should have been with the Lord'?

His naturally inquisitive mind had worried increasingly at the jigsaw pieces of his discontent until one spring day when all those pieces fell into place. No-one said anything, no-one wrote anything to him. It simply and instantly all came while he was walking the dog. The veil had been pulled back and Mark saw the real character of what was going on. He was being measured every time he was in the house-group, or the church, or anywhere in the company of any layer of the leadership. It was as if he was constantly being gauged to see if he came up to scratch on a long list of criteria that the leadership had devised. It was being done all the time.

What struck him on that early evening walk, when the curtain had been blown back, were the gauges that he was being measured with. Attendance was a pretty large gauge. Meetings per week were clocked and recorded. There were meters for length of prayer, type of Bible, clothes and voice-tone. His use – or in Mark's case, non-use – of clichés was being measured; his questioning mind, which he expressed in an innocent search for the truth, was constantly registering on another gauge – he was regarded as a potential trouble-maker, unyielding to the leadership and to God. Now he saw that never speaking in tongues publicly had placed huge, flashing neon questions over his head: 'Was this man really a Christian?' 'If so, has he quenched the Spirit?'

An ironic smile had flitted momentarily over Mark's face when he realised all this. He had been trying for months to tell himself that it wasn't really like this, that he didn't go to a church where the tradition of the leaders had assumed the status of the word of God. At least he didn't have to go on pretending to himself that the leadership wasn't really like that. But inside he felt sick.

Born again by the Spirit of God one balmy June evening on the terraces of a local football club, Mark had succumbed to the all too human desire to be accepted by taking on the likeness of what was around him. He hadn't known then that he was conforming to an image that was parochial. He hadn't known that elsewhere were Christians who lived in an atmosphere so different that it was almost a different world. But he had known what he had needed to do to fit and belong. Instinctively he knew what would give him a good score on all those gauges, even though no-one had ever mentioned them. Inflections, witty put downs, hints and innuendoes, the right books and songs, serving on the right team at church: they all gave him clear signals as to how to make the grade and fit in. Untaught as he was in the affairs of grace and faith, unschooled as he was in the matter of God's glory, he had thought that the leadership really did hear and utter the very voice of God.

Now he knew why he toiled at his Christianity. He toiled because he wanted what he felt he never had: acceptance. Mark had been trying hard, conforming more or less comfortably to the truth regime of the leaders. His sense of acceptance and worth had become completely defined by them. His direction in serving and worship had been set by them. His liberties and responsibilities, his duties and joys, holidays and friends were defined in their codes and rules. Mark had never felt accepted because he wasn't: he was assessed, not accepted.

As he took his seat the following Sunday morning he realised that he could never again believe it when the voice from the front said 'Welcome, it's great to see you this morning.'

'Where did they get their rules and codes?' Mark pondered as they moved along the usual runway of choruses and songs. The worship lifted off to the roar of the band and his mind floated back to the question: 'Where do all these rules and where does this attitude come from? Why don't I read this in my Bible?'

The congregation levelled out for a quieter song, then came the regular notices, the smartly casual Associate Pastor intoned a laid-back prayer and then, as they cruised high above the routines and realities of earth, came the sermon. He listened as never before. Now he heard the message clearly, now he could read between the lines and see not what the passage was actually saying, but what the leadership wanted to be heard: the formulae for acceptability. 'Do this and you'll fit in and then God will love you; do that and you won't and God won't really love you the way he really loves me.' As the Pastor, now energetic to the point of violence, took the sermon to a crescendo with a demand that everyone 'witness to ten new people this coming week or else you must be walking in rebellion against the Lord', Mark made his choice. Tempted though he was to switch off in cynicism and something akin to pride, he resolved to listen to another word, read another text, absorb another revelation. In that moment he chose the Lord of his conscience. And for the first time he felt that God accepted him.

What Legalism Isn't

What is it that both Abi and Mark suffer from? First we have to eliminate – as in the process of diagnosis that most doctors use – what they are *not* suffering from.

Legalism isn't a matter of having rules, boundaries or traditions in our congregations or our individual lives. Neither Abi nor Mark would be helped by a Christian life that was devoid of any rules. Both their churches need established practices and procedures, open expressions of common purpose and values, recognisable boundaries that define church life and inform holy living. While rules can be overdone, and often are by people of a certain temperament, they are necessary for good and godly order in any fellowship. God has given many laws to us in the Scriptures. He loves law. The law in the Old Testament was given by God to express his character. As his likeness was imprinted upon his people's national life, other nations would look at them and see what God was like and would worship him. Jesus came to fulfil it, not wriggle out from under it because it cramped his style. Legalism isn't the presence of rules, and the way out of legalism isn't the way of lawlessness (antinomianism, as some like to call it).

But we are tempted to think that it is. We are tempted to cry 'legalism' (like crying 'foul') whenever anyone suggests that we shouldn't do this and we really ought to do that. One whiff of a rule and we're protesting loudly, if not always out-loud.

What's going on here?

What's happening is that we are being duped. We are being duped into one of the most common mistakes that the enemy of

God's glory has taught the church: that Christian freedom is freedom to do what you want. It isn't, never has been and never will be.

Certainly that is the world's view of freedom. Outside of Christ, freedom is the absence or the overcoming of the constricting and oppressive will of others, especially God. Freedom is freedom to express yourself, choose for yourself, define and authenticate yourself. Freedom is freedom of the will-for-self: to do and think according to your own tastes, predilections, estimate of yourself and so on. It is the inseparable partner of autonomy – self-rule means freedom to choose and if need be, the freedom to exert your choice. Yet at its heart, this view of freedom is in fact as sinful as anything else, since it's not the kind of freedom for which God made us. You can trace it back to Nietzsche's 'Ubermensch', the 'Over-man' who rises over the prevailing will of all others (including God) to become fully man, fully autonomous. You can trace it further back to the figure in Greek philosophy of the happy tyrant, who is happy because he has the power to get away with whatever he wills. But if we want to read the world and ourselves biblically, it's better to trace this false view of freedom back to the Garden, to the fall: to the desire to do what's presented as being your own thing and is really the serpent's thing, and to be like a god.

Yet although we can identify its falsity, it is so easy for us to react to rules with reflexes taught by this view of freedom, as if we have a divine right never to have our style cramped or as if we are superior to all those lesser Christians who need rules. Freedom from legalism isn't freedom to do whatever we want. Down here none of us is safe to be let loose with such a freedom; our weakness or our pride couldn't cope. Up there, of course, it will be different, but up there *we* will be different!

No real good comes from this view of freedom in our churches; much wrecking of the ship of faith has happened to individuals because of it. Why such wrecking? Because the desire for autonomy can take us in two directions, both of which are away from God.

Weakness regarding sin

First, it can take us down a road that our own will is incapable of handling without us becoming caught and entangled in the net of sin. Most of us are a lot less holy than we are tempted to think: we are less strong against the tempter than he would like us to think. He would like us to be complacent about temptation. He would like us to forget that we have blind spots which prevent us from seeing our failings and weaknesses. Once we think that we are strong, then we are really weak and we become an easy target. We find sins too attractive, get into situations in which we are out of our depth and indulge tastes that become addictions. This road is called 'Weakness' because our flesh is too weak with regard to sin. We still have so much progress to make in holiness. We have not yet taken hold of that for which Christ took hold of us. We still find the same principle at work in us that worked away in Paul: 'When I want to do good, evil is right there with me.' (Rom. 7:21). We know just what it is like to find that 'what I do is not the good I want to do; no, the evil I do not want to do – this I keep on doing' (v.19). Freedom along the world's lines is no freedom, it is the path to yet deeper bondage to sin. In fact, we need rules and boundaries. Without them we don't stand a chance.

Pride regarding God

The second road that the desire for self-rule can take us down is called 'Pride'. This view of freedom as absolute autonomy reinforces our wills against God's. We do not bow in humble obedience, we rise up, bridling against others, including God. Here is no meekness, no acquiescent spirit. Here is no peace, no resting in God, no contentment. Such a Christian will never learn to be content in whatever state they find themselves. Such a Christian will find it difficult to function in the body of Christ unless they are recognised as the brain. Such a Christian will be a pain in the neck because their default setting is automatically, in a reflex kind of way, to ask 'how does this affect me?' No cross to carry, no putting others first, no love, no mind of Christ along the lines of the obedient servant of Philippians 2:6ff. And it truly is Christ who is the ultimate argument against this kind of anti-legalism, this lawlessness which is little more than anarchic pride. He submitted himself to the Father's will. He did everything that was his Father's will and he did no more than his Father's will. Whilst he rejected the 'traditions of men' he came to fulfil every last bit of every letter of God's law. He did not come to ditch the law; he did not come to show us a life without any rules. Far from grumbling, he rejoiced to do the will of the One who had sent him. Someone else's will was not a problem for him. He both shared the will of the Father and rejoiced to serve the Father. Self-rule is on the agenda of the postmodern 'over-man'; but self-rule doesn't seem to have been on the agenda of the Proper Man. The one who was strong within and strong against the foe played by the book and glorified his Father through the rules.

No lawlessness

Whatever we might think of it, legalism can't be defined as the presence of rules in the individual and shared lives of believers. If Christ, who was strong, kept God's law, can we with our many weaknesses do without law? If the perfect Son magnified the reputation of the Father through them, will we sons and daughters not also glorify our heavenly Father through the life that is ordered by them? Just as he gave the law to Israel in his grace, so he still gives that which will guide our feet along paths of holiness.

Christian freedom, therefore, isn't the absence of rules. Lawlessness – or autonomy or anarchy – is never commended in God's word. As a practice, it leads not to holiness but to chaos. As an attitude, it lies at the heart of rebellion against God. How does Scripture describe the man who leads mutiny against the most high God? The man of lawlessness. What is his other name? The son of destruction (1 Thess. 2:3). Legalism is sinful, but so also is the lawless life; so much so that 'sin is lawlessness' (1 Jn. 3:4). No surprise, then, that the devil should try and hoodwink us into running from one error into another. No surprise either that in our frailty and fickleness, and with that fallen will-to-power with which the flesh still wars against the Spirit, we should find ourselves the targets of satanic counter-intelligence. Dumping human laws, we are tricked into dumping law *per se* and thus we dump God's law and become less holy.

How many of us have found that kicking against restrictive boundaries of thought and behaviour, many of which don't deserve to be taken seriously yet with which our churches can disastrously over-abound, we have ended up cooler towards the Lord and his people? Seeing legalism as primarily a man-oriented thing, we have turned from it and the fellowship in anything other than New Testament love. In the process, we have distanced ourselves from God, not because he was even remotely in those human and often ridiculous laws but because we were striking out against his children, albeit repressive ones. Reacting against the legalities of human traditions, we encouraged within ourselves a generally lawless frame of mind. The baby of God's law – so passionately loved by psalmists – has been ditched along with the undeniably murky bathwater of man's laws. We have simply wanted to do our own thing and, in our spiritual immaturity, have extended that into not wanting to do God's thing.

So if the problem of legalism isn't simply that rules exist, and if freedom isn't freedom to do whatever you want, what's the real problem that we face?

What Legalism Is

Legalism, real legalism that creeps up on us like carbon monoxide and snuffs out our spiritual liveliness, is primarily a

God–oriented thing. As we said earlier, it's a way of making and keeping yourself acceptable to God. At its core, it is the attitude and practice of self-justification and self-sanctification. It teaches a way of righteousness and holiness that requires more dependence on this weak flesh than upon the victorious strength of Christ. It tries to provide a ground for Christian assurance which lies in ourselves and thus provides no assurance. It's a way of misusing the good laws, precepts, commandments that God in his grace builds into our lives though his word. The legalistic mind takes law and turns it into a means not of guiding and protecting life with God, but of establishing and sustaining it. It teaches you how to start the plates spinning and then how to run around frantically to keep them from falling and thus to keep the whole show going. It uses the tools of religion, it looks virtuous, it is visible and therefore gives us credibility in our fellowships. But the self-justification and self-sanctification that it teaches are deadly.

Legalism looked convincing in the past

Yet, historically, legalism has been so plausible. It was the way in which Israel became legalistic. When God rails against his own people in the early chapters of Isaiah, he speaks against people who can live in direct contradiction to God's character, yet gather in the temple and do some religion – Sabbaths and sacrifices, feasts and festivals – and assume that these observances made them acceptable to God. What God gave to guide their responsiveness to his covenant-forming grace became, in their sinful hands, tools to manipulate him into being 'gracious'. The calendar of redemptive history was turned back 430 years, as if the law were given to Moses before the promise was made with Abraham.

Even the good motive – to want to be holy by avoiding sin – provided impetus towards legalism. It was the scribes, following good Ezra, who developed 'the traditions of men'. Their interpretations and detailed, case by case applications of God's law were meant to hedge about the commandments, making it harder to break them. In itself, of course, this seems like a good idea, and we do the same thing in life nowadays. In order to avoid domestic heartache, we hedge around the command 'thou shalt not break the kitchen window' with another lesser command – 'thou shalt not play football in the back garden unless thou playest it with a soft spongy ball' and traditions – 'thou shalt take the kids to the park to play football'. Yet the elevation of the purely human interpretations and subordinate rules to the same status as the law given to Moses, turned them into the means of gaining acceptance with God.

Legalism was a huge problem in the New Testament. Arguably, Hebrews is a sustained sermon, directed against precisely this problem. The lie that was being perpetrated among the church – most likely in Jerusalem – was that in order to enjoy the benefits and blessings of the new covenant in Jesus Christ, you had to observe the ordinances of the old Mosaic covenant. This Judaizing pressure was exerted by those who dogged Paul's evangelistic and pastoral ministry. Paul reserves some of his most ballistic language for the legalistic Judaizers. Take the vocabulary that he fires off to the Galatians as an example. The Judaizers and those who were listening to them are called 'hypocrites' (2:13). They are actors, they're putting on a performance, wearing a false persona. There's nothing genuine about their spirituality and their relationship with God, it's just an act. They are 'agitators' (5:12). They are stirring up the fellowship when it should be being built up; creating storms left, right and centre when there should be an abundance of God's peace. For this teaching and its effects they are eternally condemned (1:8) – fairly strong language when you actually believe in eternal condemnation. They have a penalty to pay (5:10). Paul even comes out with the kind of language that no self-respecting Christian would dare to use in public. In one of the bluntest verses in the Bible he says 'As for those agitators, I wish they would go the whole way and emasculate themselves!'

Legalism can look convincing now

As it was, so it is. We, too, genuinely don't want sin to rule over us, we don't want to grieve God or to stray from his path. And it is a narrow path compared to the one that leads to destruction. So in order to avoid big sins we add rules to God's word – hedging sinful territory around with codes that are intended to keep us from it. We make the narrow path narrower. It's usually the well-intentioned, keen and committed, who regard sin most conscientiously, who are most susceptible to legalism. The half-hearted Christian couldn't really care enough to veer towards it, though they make up for it with many other errors.

It's also a real problem for those who are keen and insecure. Some of us love rules and regulations generally in life. Temperamentally we are disposed to that kind of living: it gives us the security of structures. Some parents are brilliant at this – something goes horribly wrong in the house, a vase is broken, and there'll be five new rules started before the kids get to bed. For new Christians – keen and somewhat insecure, children in the faith – there can be a huge susceptibility to the legalists within the fellowship. The susceptibility isn't to the right and proper guiding of a holy life that pleases the Lord and effectively witnesses to his life-changing power; it's a susceptibility to being made to feel insecure with God, to creating from the earliest months of the Christian life a pattern of behaviour and thought which seeks at best a conditional assurance, for which all the conditions have to be met by us.

It becomes plausible to us when we think that it's working. Our very ability to keep some of the house rules fuels our pride and reinforces the impression that our relationship with God is, in fact, somehow founded upon this ability. 'When I am strong, then I am strong.' Yet in the same day that we keep some of the rules we break others. Our weakness and inability to keep all of the rules feeds our despair. 'When I am weak then I am weak.' In turn, we generate more rules and make a more strenuous effort to keep them. Thus legalism both glorifies us by ascribing to us a supposed ability to reach God by our own effort, yet simultaneously reinforces our insecurities by ascribing to us insufficient ability to keep enough rules to be eternally in God's good books. Since laws and rules can be well-motivated and can be helpful, legalism seems to be on to a winner.

But of course, it isn't onto a winner. It is deadly for individuals and for fellowships. The need for order and the proper presence of rules and boundaries can just as easily feed the fallen quest for personal power. From this legalistic approach to God there inevitably flows a legalism that is directed towards one another. Legalism becomes a way of scoring sanctity points in our fellowships, and exerting a 'truth regime' – a way of controlling others by defining good and bad behaviour, and true and false ideas. It's about pride, power and control. Legalism becomes the tool for spiritual oppression and abuse, for control over others and for the elevation of our own status.

See how this pernicious kind of legalism focuses the mind on self. It takes the mind and heart away from Christ, the Proper Man. It takes our faith away from his sufficiency and wrongly places it upon ours. We live to achieve God's approval; we forget that we are already alive and accepted in Christ. Ever so plausibly, we are sold a different gospel: one that isn't really a gospel at all. The desire not to sin in some big way can be little more than a mask to hide our lack of faith in Jesus, 'who has become for us wisdom from God – that is, our righteousness, holiness and redemption' (1Cor. 1:30). Holiness becomes a matter of living on eggshells with a God who is reserving judgement on us and might turn us away at any moment.

It really is a false and deadly thing, this warped alternative, this lie, this all-pervasive and hideous distortion of Christian living.

Is There a Cure?

Can we be free from such an endemic and destructive ailment?
If the disease has always dogged the life of the church, is there
any real hope of totally eradicating it, or do we just have to
accept that just as there will always be sin down here on earth,
so we will always encounter this particular form of it until we
reach heaven? Will it always be a plague upon God's new
society until his people are glorified? I suspect that the church
will, in fact, keep suffering and causing others to suffer from
legalism. It reflects a current of our fallen-ness which run so
deep and strong that the problem will recurrently flood its
banks. But all is not lost.

In 1981 my back 'went'. Young, fit and healthy though I was
at the time, and though I made a good recovery from the initial problem, back pain will probably always be with me down
here. I might have fairly infrequent episodes nowadays, since
I've learned to adapt my lifestyle somewhat. But my back can
go into spasm without warning and while I'm performing perfectly normal manoeuvres. When it does, the most simple
movements seem to belong to a different life – how could I
possibly have ever climbed those stairs, fed those rabbits or
driven that car?

Like the church's weak back, legalism is a feature of life
before glory: it's part of the 'not yet' in which we are called to
live and struggle and gain victories. Celestial fruits do grow on
earthly ground; but it is very earthly ground.

Like a weak back, legalism can be dealt with to such a degree
that it rarely plagues us. We might suffer its spasms, our fellowships might find a sudden onslaught of pride and might succumb
to the obstinate human trait of self-justification. There is also
always a devil prowling around seeking whom he may devour.
We might never, on earth, have a total eradication of the condition. Yet for the soul that wants them, there are cures to be had
from the great physician of souls. While we might not be able to

wipe it out totally from life down here, we have not been left without remedies that make it an infrequent problem, ease the pain when we do suffer, and enable otherwise crippled saints to walk and run and dance with joy in God. There is help. It is such wonderful help that this awful, debilitating, deadly illness, which can grip us like a vice, becomes no longer the norm but rather the thing from which once we suffered and now with which we are only occasionally bothered. Deliverance from a life commanded by legalism is a wonderful thing. It brings hope for fellowships and renewal for the individual. God, in his infinite grace and mercy, gives us a way to live so that his glory and our desire for it drives away the darkness and floods earth with heaven's light. So that we can learn to see the problem more clearly, hate it properly and find its cures, we turn now to examine the texture and deadliness of legalism in more detail. As we do, we will take in the biblical cures: they are wonderful, liberating and suffused with God's grace, true faith and the glory of God.

2

Legalism is Useless ...

One of legalism's most secure hooks into the Christian life is that it appears to work. It looks like a practical, effective solution to our spiritual problems. Only it doesn't work. In Scripture we have repeated appeals to see the uselessness of the legalistic life at precisely those points where it is presented to us as being so useful. I want us to explore two areas in life where it seems to be just the thing that we need, but in fact is the last thing that we need. As we see how it cannot touch the problem of sin, and cannot bring us any closer to God, we are brought to remedies that might at first sight appear to be unappealing: a true picture of sin and a bigger view of the holiness of God. Yet as these remedies clarify the inadequacy of legalism, they point us to the wonderful adequacy of God.

Useless Against Sin

It seems remarkable to those that naturally veer towards a legalistic life, but legalism cannot deal with sin. As a means of gaining the principal deliverance which every child of Adam needs, and in the principal battle to which every Christian is called, legalism is useless. It is a complete waste of time and effort: futile. Legalism as a way of breaking the power of sin and of living with God is utterly useless for non-Christians and Christians alike.

Why?

Law can't reach the heart

In the first place, law never reaches the well-spring of the heart. Law is not bad, as we've seen, but it's not good enough to get down to the core of our being and change us there. However stringently we and our fellowships apply both God's law and ours, we can only ever apply them. They are only ever external measures. As such, they can have an effect upon us that might seem to be making us holy. We might have certain aspects of our behaviour curbed that otherwise would be damaging to others and even to ourselves, but on the inside we still hanker after a good old sin. The well-spring of the heart is not cleansed and purified by law, it's simply diverted along better paths. Our nature is not changed by the law. The law might persuade us of the need to change, but it can never actually effect the change that we so desperately need. Law can never rob sin of its capacity and power to entangle you, beset you, command you or distance you from God.

In fact sin and death are more powerful than law. Sin, in its hold over us before we were saved, robbed the law of any power to change us from rebellious sinners to children of God. Sin blocked any progress of the law into the core of our lives where it might make our hearts righteous. And yes, even now God's law, his holy and righteous law by which he expresses his own perfect character so that the people who are his by faith might in turn express that character to the watching world – even this law is useless against the residue of sin that lurks within.

We need the Bible to teach us that, of course. Left to ourselves, we might foster the delusion that simply by keeping laws we are doing well with God, that we are better than we really are. We might fondly imagine that because we'd kept seven out of ten (for at least half an hour) we were doing pretty well with the commandments. And if our perception of how we are with God is based upon this, we'll be 70 per cent of the way there and only a pretty unreasonable examiner would fail us for that! But the Bible says our sin has debilitated the law, rendering it impotent as an agent of personal change. No matter how religious we might be, we face death as much as ever if we rely on the law to give us life. God had to do something for us in Christ and by the Spirit in order to break that power. Thus Romans 8:3: '… what the law was powerless to do in that it was weakened by the sinful nature, God did by sending his own Son…' In case these Christians in Rome had missed the point, and using the language (somewhat indelicately, to our contemporary ears) of circumcision, Paul later talks about the inward work upon the heart. Thus Romans 2:28-29: 'A man is not a Jew if he is only one outwardly, nor is circumcision merely outward and physical. No, a man is a Jew if he is one inwardly; and circumcision is circumcision of the heart, by the Spirit, not by the written code'. The life that is legalistic is the life that is weak against sin and death.

Now this has an obvious consequence for non-Christians who seek to get right with God by doing enough to inherit eternal life. They can't. The awful tragedy of nominal Christianity is that it leaves people dead in their transgressions and sins. Legalism's particular deadliness is that it can give the appearance of life. Like a puppet, the non-Christian makes movements that can look like there's life there. But cut the strings of law – by any means you choose – and the caricature of life collapses into a heap of painted wood. This thing was never alive. It was never regenerate and justified.

But there's a more covert consequence for believers. To think that we can give our holiness strength through laws merely leaves us prone to the weakness of our hearts. We are still frail against sin. We may have the appearance of fortitude but in truth the spring of action, the heart, is still feeble. Not surprising, is it, that legalistic fellowships can harbour adultery, power-plays and cruelties of all kinds? Neither should it surprise us that legalistic individuals can fall prey to the sudden onslaught of temptation and fail catastrophically. This saint was never strong. His legalism worked to perpetuate, not challenge, the weaknesses within. The stains of death still seep through 'holy' clothes.

Law can't foil the tempter

Secondly, law is useless against the tempter – jings, he'll use it! No law defeated him. No written code could ever rob him of his strength, bind the strong man, plunder his domain, crush his head and release his captives. So if you wear the chiffon 'armour' of legalism in your battles against the tempter, you're in for a hammering. You might think that you're safe if you make a rule never to be in a room alone with an attractive member of the opposite sex. But that rule can never curb lust and it cannot protect you from the sharp and sudden ferocity of the tempter. Law never cast out Satan, never rebuked him, never humiliated him, never vanquished him. It took God the Son, a cross and an empty grave to do these things.

We forget this at our peril. Partly, I think, because the whole notion of spiritual warfare has either dropped out of our idealised Christian lifestyle or else has become so dramatised that we are numbed to its normality. It belongs to Christian novels about 'the end times', it requires weird jargon, violent praying; it's something we think of only when we're in a spiritual tizz, stirred up into an emotionally agitated state by the church leaders speaking too close to the microphone. By such devious means the enemy has us duped into unawareness the rest of the time. What's spiritual warfare got to do with the weekly shop at the supermarket, the school run, the business lunch? We keep the church rules, some of God's rules as well, and forget that the enemy is craftier than we are. As a shield, our legalism is too small and flimsy. If the heart is weak we are soft targets. Where is our strength against the tempter? Not in our own powers of law-keeping but in Christ alone. Ephesians 6:10 says 'be strong in the Lord and in his mighty power.' As Martin Luther wrote in his hymn *A Safe Stronghold*, 'The Lord's Sabaoth's son, he and no other one, shall conquer in the battle'.

Law can't wipe out guilt

In the third place, legalism cannot deal with sin because it cannot yield forgiveness. The laws are the very written, or in some cases insidiously unspoken, codes that a person breaks. Break the law at only one point and you stand condemned by the law. Law cannot declare to sinners a word of forgiveness, it only declares offence, guilt, condemnation. In fact, by adding self-sufficiency to our list of iniquities, it actually compounds our guilt. Romans again, this time 3:20, says 'Therefore no-one will be declared righteous in his sight by observing the law.' Try and cover your sin with a period of enhanced law-keeping and what happens? You can't deal with sin; you can't approach God and you fall away from the experiencing of God's grace. But it gets worse. You lose your assurance. The one who is glorified in forgiving is denied glory and you reinforce a fruitless pattern of response to sin.

Despite this, so often we do try and claw our way back into God's good books and back to our comfortable condition by good works. Preferring to think that our sin isn't really so bad that it needs mere forgiveness, we persuade ourselves – and in this much of our legalistic evangelicalism, of whatever shade, conspires – that we can fix it. There is something about the destitution and helplessness of the fallen saint that we'd rather avoid. To cast ourselves utterly upon the mercy and grace of God, to come to him for forgiveness rather than for approval is difficult. Forgiveness is humbling – not humiliating, but certainly humbling. Forgiveness brings me to an end of myself, to a death.

With respect to sin's power, author and penalty, legalism is useless. It is simply unable to clear away the barriers and bridge the chasm between us and God. Hebrews 7:19 states: 'for the law made nothing perfect.' And this ought not to surprise us, for God never intended that it should do these things. He never justified anyone on the basis of the works of the law. Like the Galatian Christians, we need to be reminded of this. We put the history the wrong way round, forgetting that in fact the law came 430 years after God made a covenant of grace and promise with Abraham. Putting the cart before the horse, we put law before grace as if Sinai came first. He who had not even heard of Moses was justified; he was justified by his faith. It's the only way. The righteous shall live by faith. Yet the fog of legalism blinds us to the transparently clear truth of God's word. The false security that we can feel seems more comfortable than casting ourselves upon God's mercy. Why trust someone you can't see when you can *do* something? But what we *do* is in vain.

No Nearer to God

Bleak as it might sound, the problem of uselessness against sin is only part of the awfulness of the disease of legalism. Precisely because it cannot deal with sin, it cannot bring us nearer to God.

Climbing God's hill

Take Psalm 24 for example. The question is put to the worshippers – maybe two choirs singing question and answer here – 'Who may ascend the hill of the LORD? Who may stand in his holy place?' The natural answer for us, in our affirming days, is 'We all may, every one of us – come on up, you're welcome as you are.' Mmmmm. This is not the answer sung by choir number two. Who can come close to God? Who can dwell in his presence? Remember that Israel was warned not even to go near Sinai when God came down to the summit. So now that God's name dwells in Zion, who can ascend? The answer is not encouraging to anyone, but especially not to legalists, like those in Abi's church, before whose eyes appears a ladder of rule-rungs. 'He who has clean hands and a pure heart, who does not lift up his soul to an idol or swear by what is false.' This is bad news. The law will not bring you nearer to God because you break the law. By sin you break each rung that you try to climb on.

Our legalistic fellowships – of whatever ilk they might be – merely multiply reasons for *not* ascending the hill of God. In them we are constantly constrained to cry 'Unclean hands, impure heart!' Our hearts endlessly forge idols and each fresh production run cries 'Keep away from the true and living God.' This is not the same as being sensitive to sin, it's a matter of where our trust is placed. By unwittingly placing our trust in what is actually a broken ladder we neglect the one whose hands were clean for us, whose heart was pure and in whom there was neither idolatry nor misplaced accountability. We keep our distance from God the Son who came and went back – who ascended the hill of God for us. We do not enjoy the blessing of the 'King of glory', 'the LORD strong and mighty, the LORD mighty in battle.' And the blessing is proximity to God.

Suppose that in your church the message is either stated or just subliminally inferred that you can come close to God by keeping the house rules about drinking wine. (In some fellow-ships this will mean not drinking, in others this will mean not abstaining!) By keeping the rule you are allowed by God to draw near to him. By breaking it you are barred from your Father's presence. It needn't be drinking wine, of course: it might be wearing a hat if you're a woman; it might be dressing smartly – or casually, depending on your fellowship. It might be your meeting attendance score sheet; it might be whether you raise your hands when singing. The list is tragically endless. The message sounds plausible: Do good and God will welcome you. But it's deadly in its falsehood. Why? Because it leaves aside the One who alone brings us to God, and thus leaves supposedly weak Christians – who are defined as such because they have (or haven't) slurped a glass since last week – distanced from God.

It's not such a ludicrous scene. It's commonplace, and it was in the early church. It wasn't claret or clothing that was the problem, it was eating meat that might have been offered to an idol by the butcher before he slapped it on the counter. Thus God needed to get Paul to write to the church in Corinth that the matter of food had importance in terms of weakness and strength of conscience and in terms of thoughtfulness, building up your neighbour and not showing off; but in regard to the food itself bringing you closer to God, the food was irrelevant. Thus 1 Corinthians 8:8 says 'But food does not bring us near to God; we are no worse if we do not eat, and no better if we do.'

But as with the power, author and penalty of sin, so with nearness to God. It's not simply that legalism can't create it, it's also that legalism masks the lack of it.

Spoiling prayer

Nowhere is this more keenly the case than in that realm in which we draw near to God most deliberately and consciously: the realm of prayer. It's almost as big a source of Christian neuroses as witnessing, yet prayer is meant to be the most precious privilege and the most effective work that we can possibly enjoy down here.

Prayer is where we meet heaven. It's where we enter the most holy place on the assuredly rock-solid ground of the new and living way opened up for us. Standing on Christ-ground, as it were, we stand in the very presence of God. With both intimacy and relaxed familiarity, yet with the most profound awe and respect, we call the Maker of heaven and earth whose righteousness is as fire, 'Father'. It's the realm where sores are healed, where the balm of grace flows over us. It's the place where the searchlight of truth shines into the deepest recesses of our souls, yet is only destructive for the sin that loiters there. It's the place where I can cry and be understood perfectly, where I can be tired without being impolite, for if I cannot find rest in God's presence where can I find it? It's the place where I can be angry safely, can moan without being chucked out, can be guided, calmed, filled with joy, imbued with resolve, filled with the Spirit, sing, be silent, sleep in perfect peace like a child. All this because it's the realm of fellowship with God. Here I am before the face of Jehovah. Here I am as close to home as I'm ever going to be on earth. Here I see more of the glory than anywhere else on earth; here I'm turned inside out to God; here I'm a listener and here my voice is heard. Here is no place for pretence before my all-seeing Creator; here is no place for acting, for wearing the mask of piety. Here, no self-righteousness can stand. Yet here legalism can be at its most potent.

Will he not turn away from me because of my sin? Doesn't the Bible say that if I regard – cherish – iniquity in my heart he will not hear me? Yes. And doesn't the Bible say that without holiness no-one will see the Lord? Yes. But legalism isn't the answer to my sin. The death and resurrection of Jesus Christ is the answer to it. He alone has cleared and repeatedly clears the rubble that lies between me and God. God's work of redemption, not my works of self-justification, bring me closer to God. Grace and faith, not law and flesh bring me near.

Perhaps no better place to see it is in the verses that were alluded to above, from Hebrews 10:19ff. The big theological question for those who had grown up in a first century Jewish background was arguably not a political one to do with the Romans, but was a matter that we would call a prayer problem. How do you come near to God? How could you be properly represented by the High Priest? How could you get close to that bit of the temple that was the place where the Holy One of Israel came down? How could you be on the right side of God? It was an acute question for every pious Jew – it still is. How do you create the access and having access, how do you make the approach?

The stark answer was that you couldn't. Under the old covenant only the high priest could go through the curtain that separated unholy humanity from the real and glorious presence of the holy God. That curtain stood for sinful flesh – it said 'no sinner can enter'. The most holy place was fenced off, veiled; God the Most Holy was too dangerous for sinners to be near. Only once a year, on the Day of Atonement, could the high priest enter with the blood of the atoning sacrifice upon him as a protection – as it had been on the doorposts of Israel's houses in Egypt on the night of the last, fatal plague.

The encouragement for these Hebrew Christians is also a plea – don't go back to that way. Don't go back to the old covenant's inaccessibility and inapproachability. For, wonder of wonders, in Christ who in his flesh took our sinfulness and in whom our sinful flesh was judged, flesh is no longer a barrier but now in him – in this incarnate man – there is an open door, a new and living way *in*, through the curtain torn upon the cross. Now in Christ you have access. So make the approach. Don't go back to the way of the curtain; go on and in with Christ who is the new and living way into the very presence of God. Pray!

This exhortation rescues our praying from legalism. Christ is all our access; in him we can approach. Now, we don't need to crack any codes. Christ has fulfilled everything for us; he has made the proper sacrifice for sin, and in him the distance between me and God is overcome. My mobile phone can be blocked from connecting to certain kinds of number. It's known as 'call barring'. One of the reasons that the network can bar my calls is if I haven't paid the monthly fee. However accurately I dial the barred numbers, I'll never get through. I only get a message on the screen which reminds me of the call barring. Legalism is my attempt to pay the price to remove the call barring from prayer. But Christ has removed it on the cross. Now I can speak to God in prayer, calling upon him in the day of my trouble. In Christ, we do not need to try and remove the call barring by performing of the duties of religion. In Christ we have a clear line, even if the first call we might need to make is to say we're sorry.

But don't we treat prayer in precisely this way? Don't we talk about 'breaking through'? Don't we feel the need to qualify? I still wrestle with the cooling off period. I come to God in remorse and repentance. I ask for his free forgiveness. But then I behave as if I was unworthy of receiving any blessing until a decent time has elapsed, a qualifying time. Even in prayer I seek to justify my presence in God's presence with a little bit of payment, a little bit of penance. 'I can't ask you for anything Lord because it's only half an hour since I had to repent for swearing at the cat – give me another ten minutes and then I'll be fit for you to bless me again.'

Legalism and the prayer meeting

We go back to the curtain with our long public prayers; we do the Pharisaic bit that Jesus warned the disciples against: thinking that we'll be heard for our many words. We do it when we carefully craft our 'choice' prayers. They may be the sweetly sentimental ones, they might be the trendily urbane and cleverly sophisticated ones, or the violently assaulting ones (assaulting God, I mean!), or the ones where we eloquently recap a very big book of systematic theology without hesitation, deviation or repetition but definitely not in just a minute. We do it and we subliminally teach it in our prayer meetings with the tones of voice, the unwritten lists of acceptable subject matter … We turn our prayer meetings into performances, we pray to the gallery.

In so doing, we intimidate the quiet and sensitive, we silence the weak, the inexperienced, the broken, the doubtful and the stranger who doesn't understand the codes. We keep out the faltering honesty and the pain, the ignorance and the weakness. We establish something with the form of closeness to God by a thousand and one traditions of men and works of the law. And in doing this our legalistic prayers create a false proximity, discourage real intimacy and can so easily mask our actual distance. They do so in our prayer meetings, and they do so even more perniciously when we are on our own with God and yet still wear the mask.

In the realm of nearness to God – as a controller of where we stand with the Holy One and as a regulator of the enjoyment of fellowship with God – legalism is a killer. But mercifully it is a killer that faces a surprising antidote.

3

... So Swap Legalism for Truth

To break the grip of legalistic attempts to deal with sin and bring us closer to God we need what might seem to be the least likely counter-measure. The legalistic mind has too shallow a view of sin and too small a grasp of the holiness of God. To rid yourself of the effects of legalism you need a deeper view of sin and greater awe before the Holy One.

The Awful Truth About Sin

Why is this so? The great presupposition behind a legalistic route to holiness is that by rules you can stamp out the spread of sin. It reasons that it can deal with sin by adding a few rules to the commands of Scripture (more than a few, if they seem to be required: there's no shortage). But as we've already noted, the law of Moses was powerless against sin. Laws can curb the sinful behaviour of the sinner, but can never stop us wanting to sin, which is itself a sin. They can make bad people behave better, but they can't make bad people good. So to rid ourselves of legalism's attitudes and presuppositions, there's nothing quite like an understanding of the depths of the impact and power of sin. To see its horror and the strength of its grip, to see our own sinful susceptibility to it, to gaze down the canyon into which mankind has fallen, is to awaken a Christian to their inability to deal with it themselves.

Sin is more than skin-deep

It was the classic mistake the of Scribes and Pharisees to see sin as only skin deep. They had managed, with remarkable creativity, to reduce righteousness to a series of technicalities. If you got the procedures and the paperwork right, you fulfilled all righteousness. We are equally adept at doing this. Denominations are brilliant at it. With our committees and meetings and carefully detailed procedures, getting the right paperwork in the right place at the right time is crucial to getting anything done. The proper form (in both senses: the proper procedure and the proper bit of paper) is the key to acceptable practice in the church. But it can so easily be seen as the key to that which is acceptable to the God who made the church. The logic is impressively institutional.

The problem with that kind of reasoning is that if you define righteousness in legal, procedural terms, you do the same with its opposite: sin. Take one part of the Sermon on the Mount, for instance. In Jesus' day getting a divorce was simply a matter of filling in the right form. The actual reason for divorce was immaterial: as long as you followed the right procedure, you were okay, before the Pharisees and before God. No matter if you were ditching your wife (yes, only men could divorce) merely because she burnt the cakes or looked a little less pretty than when you were first betrothed (and considerably less pretty than that more recent model from the wealthy home a few streets away). No matter if you had failed to love and cherish your wife: if she displeased you over what time the tea was on the table or how clean the home was when you brought your friends home, you could divorce her – as long as you got the paperwork right. You could mistreat this woman whom you were supposed to cherish and honour; you could wound and disgrace this girl who wanted and needed the security that you could give. You could betray the trust that she and her family had shown in you. You could treat her like a mere possession, she whom God had made for his glory, this covenant child of God most high. You could sin against her and against her parents and against her Maker. As long as you got the paperwork right …

You see what happens? When you make righteousness a matter of the surface appearance, you thereby make sin the same. You make both superficial. So sin becomes a superficial problem, with no root in the heart. If it's all a matter of the details of behaviour, then you can solve it yourself with a few (hundred) rules. But it's like taking a paracetamol for cancer.

Notice the consequence of making sin superficial: you ignore its real corrupting power within and you actually end up protecting it. By confining the correction of the soul to the external and codified life, you leave the corruption of the heart unaddressed. You give corruption a safe and untouched haven. The storms of law can rage on the outside, while the sinfulness of the heart goes unchallenged, unmolested, strong. That's why some of the most legalistic people can be the worst, harbouring hideously wicked attitudes and practices. Thus the legalists, the Scribes and the Pharisees, put God's Son to death. It's why you can strain at a gnat and swallow a camel. It's why you can have a whitewashed sepulchre.

Scripture's account of deep-seated sin

Satan was the most subtle creature in the garden. By a few semantic tricks he deceived Adam and Eve from their sinless state and from Eden. He is a principality and a power that holds nations and empires. He corrupts and perverts truth, making it into a lie. He twists human behaviour into the very opposite of what God made it to be. From the fall onwards, unholiness has spiralled through humanity like a defining gene. Switched this way or that by our environment, it has coursed its way from Eden to wher-ever you are sitting as you read this book. From the first generation after that exiled pair, humanity was spoiled from the inside out and from the heart came rebellion rather than worship. The created relationship was exchanged for its opposites.

With Moses up the mountain and the thunders of God around Sinai's summit, the evil in the hearts of the people turned them away to idolatry – and Jehovah only a few hundred metres away! That corruption would characterise their life in the land until the exile of Judah. God knew it and repeatedly warned his people of its consequences before they even set foot in Canaan. From Deuteronomy 17 to 24 we have no fewer than nine commands from God to 'purge the evil from among you'. Once there, with the commands and all the ceremonial laws in place, they descended into the kind of amorality that we find so alarm-ing in our culture today: 'Everyone did what was right in his own eyes' (Judg. 21:5). Not 'everyone did stuff that was wrong even though they knew it to be wrong'. It was much worse. They redefined right and wrong according to their own whims and desires. 'If you want to do it, it must be right. Throw off God; do what seems right to you.' Heard that recently?

Led by evil king after evil king, the people willingly fol-lowed. The sin wasn't just some external pressure, a fault of the leaders, a product of the environment and culture, a necessity. Evil happened because people wanted that which was evil. 'The heart is deceitful above all things, and desperately sick; who can understand it? (Jer. 17:9 ESV). The word *anash* in the Hebrew is a medical term. The Authorised Version translates it as des-perately wicked; 'wicked' might be better known, but *anash* is better rendered 'sick'.

Jesus pressed this point home to the legalists of his day. Sin came from the heart and the remedies had to be applied there, not least of which was the need to recognise the inadequacy of a superficial – surface only – view of sin. Thus he tore the blindfolds from the disciples, who had learned so much from the Scribes and the

Pharisees and who needed to unlearn it all if they were going to follow him. 'Are you still so dull?' Jesus asked them.

> Don't you see that whatever enters the mouth goes into the stomach and then out of the body? But the things that come out of the mouth come from the heart, and these make a man 'unclean'. For out of the heart come evil thoughts, murder, adultery, sexual immorality, theft, false testimony, slander. These are what make a man 'unclean'; but eating with unwashed hands does not make him 'unclean' (Mt.15:16-20).

He taught his disciples, then and now, to pray that they would not be led into evil but would be delivered from the evil one. He prayed it himself in his great 'high priestly prayer' in John 17: 'My prayer is not that you take them out of the world but that you protect them from the evil one (Jn. 17:15).

Paul demolishes the argument that we are basically good and need only a few laws to become acceptable to God. He closes his relentless analysis of evil in the human heart in Romans 1-3 with the categorical descriptions of man found in the Psalms.

> As it is written: 'There is no-one righteous, not even one; there is no-one who understands, no-one who seeks God. All have turned away, they have together become worthless; there is no-one who does good, not even one.' ... Their throats are open graves; their tongues practise deceit ... The poison of vipers is on their lips ...Their mouths are full of cursing and bitterness ... Their feet are swift to shed blood; ruin and misery mark their ways, and the way of peace they do not know ... There is no fear of God before their eyes. (Rom. 3:10-18)

As the saying goes, 'we're not sinners because we sin, we sin because we're sinners.' Thus he concludes: 'Therefore no-one will be declared righteous in his sight by observing the law' (verse 20). Sin is inside us; quite naturally we love it; and it comes out from the inside. Even when we're Christ's, we find it working within us – like a spiritual law of gravity that always drags us down, away from heaven.

> I know that nothing good lives in me, that is, in my sinful nature. For I have the desire to do what is good, but I cannot carry it out. For what I do is not the good I want to do; no, the evil I do not want to do – this I keep on doing. Now if I do what I do not want to do, it is no longer I who do it, but it is sin living in me that does it. So I find this law at work: when I want to do good, evil is right there with me (Rom. 7:18-21).

Sin should send us to Christ

The Bible tells us that a superficial view of sin is hopelessly inadequate as a diagnosis of the human condition, and legalism is useless against it. Shake your church rule book at sin and Satan laughs in derision. Legalism should quake before the biblical teaching about sin. For in his grace God has given us the truth about sin and it should be enough to drive us not to the rule book, but to Christ. What but the truth of God can penetrate the heart, lay bare the nature as sinful, reveal the truth about us and our sin? What but the power of God can break the power of sin? What but the victory of Christ can free us from our captivity to sin? What but the life of God can overcome the deadliness of sin? Next to this, the legalist's regulations look ridiculously feeble and miss the point with criminal stupidity. We should abandon any attempt to deal with sin by rules when we see it for what it is. The truth about it is awful enough to drive us to the Lord of grace by faith.

But this might not be enough. So there is more to help us to release our own grip on self-sufficiency, and thereby disable legalism's grip on us, by the flip side of the truth abut sin: the truth about the holiness of God.

The awesome holiness of God

Legalism can't touch sin; neither can it meet the holiness of
God. It only takes a few moments to think about this one. Abi
and Mark can help here.

The right clothes

In her pre-Ed days, Abi kept the church rules about clothing.
She was coming into the presence of God to worship him along
with his people. Her fellowship prized reverence and respectabil-
ity – the latter just a teensy-weensy bit more than the former. So
as not to offend the Almighty or the elders, she had to put on
her best clothes. Dressing up in this way showed that she was not
treating the majestic God with contempt but with reverence.
After all, reasoned the church leaders, wouldn't Abi get dressed
up to go and see the Queen? Her Sunday clothes demonstrated,
so they said, that her heart was right before the Holy One.

Mark's church leaders knew that the Lord sees not as man
sees, for man looks on the outward appearance but the Lord
looks on the heart. So, they reasoned, it doesn't matter what you
look like, within the bounds of decency. (Besides, it's such a has-
sle having to get all togged up just for church, especially when
you're going to change into something more comfortable the
moment you get home.) They rightly taught what seemed to be
a liberating doctrine: that God accepts us just as much when we
are still in our pyjamas an hour before the service as he does
when we're clothed and in our right minds during the service.
But despite the liberating doctrine that was taught from the
front, or at least in the house group, it soon became apparent that
if Mark did get all dressed up the leadership thought that he was
in bondage to a legalistic spirit. Mark realised that he'd better
make himself acceptable to the fellowship and show that he
could keep himself right with God. He learned to put his jeans
back on after Saturday night – if only he could find them …

Which fellowship is the legalistic one when it comes to the question of what to wear when worshipping the Holy One? They are both equally so! What I can or can't wear on the Lord's day, going to the cinema, listening to rock music, enjoying wine, keeping up the church attendances, witnessing, whatever; we think that these decrees actually work a kind of 'survivability' before God.

Are we daft? Have we completely lost sight of the holiness of God? The legalist has.

How does this insanity work? Let's play it out a little. I dress in a manner that will gain God's approval and make my singing and praying more acceptable. But maybe I have harboured uncharitable, vaguely murderous thoughts toward my neighbour whose dog was barking half the night. I do not love my neighbour as myself. So God, in all the infinite splendour of his holiness, who cannot look upon sin, who dwells in perfect light, who sees to the very depths of my soul and who knows every thought and word, thinks what? Do I imagine either that he's impressed by my suit – or that he is impressed by my relaxed attitude – and awards me brownie points? Do I fondly imagine that he weighs the 'good' bits which my rule-keeping has provided against my bad bits? And as he watches the scale tipped down on the good side by my rule-keeping, he declares me to be righteous in his sight? Is that how it works?

We know that it is not so, but the legalist functions as if it were. He creates an 'un-holy' God. He fashions a God who is not absolutely different from us. Jehovah becomes just a bigger version of us and not actually God. Functioning as we do, this God, so this mindset assumes, is satisfied with a few more ticks than crosses on our list. What is he? Our personal and personalised divine accountant, who tots up the credits and the debits and gives a plus or minus balance? 'Oh, I'm a little bit overdrawn with my God this month so I'd better put in a few more moral pounds to bring me back up.' You have to think something like that to carry on in the legalistic life.

Glimpsing the holiness of God

I've known some legalists in my time, and the one thing that has struck me about them is that none of them have ever known God in the way that brings silence and awe-struck reverence. Except, perhaps, those for whom the legalism is too strongly driven by fear-without-trust; who have a sense of God's great and terrible holiness but are motivated to try and meet it with more rule keeping. But get one glimpse of the holiness of God, one tiny, brief glimpse, and any notion of personally created adequacy shrivels, withered and scorched by the absolute and uncompromising holiness that threatened to break out upon Israel at Sinai.

> Moses said to the LORD, "The people cannot come up Mount Sinai, because you yourself warned us, 'Put limits around the mountain and set it apart as holy.'" The LORD replied, "Go down and bring Aaron up with you. But the priests and the people must not force their way through to come up to the LORD, or he will break out against them." So Moses went down to the people and told them (Ex. 19:23-25).

Listen to those who saw and knew his works 'Ascribe to the LORD the glory due to his name. Bring an offering and come before him; worship the LORD in the splendour of his holiness. Tremble before him, all the earth!' (1 Chr. 16:29-30 with echoes in Psalms 29 and 96).

See Isaiah in the Temple, prostrate before the thrice holy one – the holiest one. See the four living creatures again in heavenly temple in Revelation 4:8; 'Day and night they never stop saying: "Holy, holy, holy is the Lord God Almighty, who was, and is, and is to come."'

Hear the prophetic word of promised redemption through Isaiah, in whose prophesy Jehovah is most frequently called the

Holy One of Israel: 'When they see among them their children, the work of my hands, they will keep my name holy; they will acknowledge the holiness of the Holy One of Jacob, and will stand in awe of the God of Israel' (Is. 29:23).

Hear those who are victorious in heaven as they sing 'the song of Moses the servant of God and the song of the Lamb:

> "Great and marvellous are your deeds, Lord God Almighty. Just and true are your ways, King of the ages. Who will not fear you, O Lord, and bring glory to your name? For you alone are holy. All nations will come and worship before you, for your righteous acts have been revealed" (Rev. 15:3-4).

Now ask yourself whether such a feeble thing as our legalistic 'righteousness' could last a moment before such a God? He is great and terrible in his holiness. He is to be feared and trusted, not negotiated with. The holiness of God should crush any confidence in the legalistic life. It's no way to live with our God. There is only one way to live with God, and that is by faith in Jesus Christ who is 'our righteousness, holiness and redemption' (1 Cor. 1:30). Nothing less than the blood of Christ can cover the guilt and shame of sin. Nothing but the righteousness of Christ will enable us to stand in the presence of the Holy One. In him and in him alone can we, whose hands are anything but clean and whose hearts are anything but pure 'ascend the hill of the Lord'. Only 'by the blood of Jesus, by a new and living way opened for us through the curtain, that is, his body', can we enter the Most Holy Place and approach God (Heb. 10:19-20).

4

Legalism's False Gospel ...

The gospel is good news. I don't just meant that the Greek word *euangelion* means 'good news', I mean that the message of the person and the work of Jesus Christ, in whom the sovereign, redeeming God has gained, purely out his grace and mercy, salvation for us from the guilt, penalty and power of sin – this gospel really is the best news that there is. Whether or not the world in its badness recognises it as such is another matter; but the opinion of the world is not the arbiter here.

The gospel communicates that which changes lives and can preserve societies. It can give hope to the hopeless, joy to the downcast, purpose to the aimless, significance to the downtrodden and the unnoticed. The gospel proclaims the power of God to heal broken lives and rescue from their own prisons those who are captive to sin. The gospel, this unparalleled good news, might be foolishness and offensive to the world, but it is the power of God for salvation. The church didn't invent it, she merely testifies by means of it. When she preaches it, the Spirit that gives life accompanies it with regenerating power. God and the angels rejoice when, because of its proclamation, rebel souls repent, prodigals are reconciled to God, the spiritually dead are brought to newness of life and proud hearts bow in humble worship.

It is such good news that people live, suffer and die to tell it, contending with hell in its cause. Its truth burns in the souls of believers and ignites a fire of passionate witness and faithful testimony. People love this more than their own lives. This message reaches across generations, crosses continents, transcends language barriers, unites warring enemies. There is no news like it in all the earth. It is good news from heaven, where the very best that earth can produce is eclipsed by the infinite splendour and brilliance of the new-creating love of almighty God. The preaching of the eternal gospel is the primary task of the church on earth; the glory that comes to God from the gospel is the primary focus of the church in heaven. By the preaching of the gospel, a great multitude that no-one can count, from every nation, tribe, people and language, will stand before the throne and in front of the Lamb and cry out in a loud voice: 'Salvation belongs to our God, who sits on the throne, and to the Lamb.'

Great, indeed, is the gospel of our glorious God. Hallelujah!

It is God's revealed message, not man's made up message. The gospel is as complete, as finished, as the saving work it proclaims. To subtract from the gospel is to imply that we need less than the work that it proclaims; to add to it is to imply some kind of insufficiency in that work Either way, the truth is opposed by fallacy.

Which brings us to this second angle on the deadliness of legalism. It's not only useless, it's worse than useless: it perverts the gospel. The legalistic voice preaches a different gospel which is really no gospel at all. It is a false gospel in two senses ...

False Gospel? Bad news!

In the first sense, it's a false, non-gospel because it replaces the grace of God with a combination of grace and works. The devil has always shown subtlety and in this distortion of the gospel he is true to form. Again, we can see the nature of the problem as we read Galatians.

Legalism in Galatia: grace isn't quite enough

Approached by Judaizers, some of the Christians in Galatia had been persuaded by the arguments that were presented to them. They live on in one form or another and it's instructive for us to understand what was going on in the early church so soon after the resurrection, so soon after the gospel of God, the gospel of grace, had been so fruitfully preached. Who were these people against whom Paul deploys some of his strongest language?

Almost certainly they were not simply Jews who were bound tight in legalism, determined to stamp out the church and re-establish a way to God based on doing all the works that the law of Moses (and all the scribal interpretations and additions) required. For one thing, it's inaccurate and simplistic to tar all the Jews of Paul's day with the brush of legalism. There were first-century Jews who believed in the inadequacy of righteous acts as a basis for prayer, preferring the basis of the abundant mercies of the sovereign God. But theirs was not the only view; the Jews of Paul's day were no more homogenous in their beliefs than the Jews of ours. From what they each said, it is clear that Jesus and Paul encountered a deep, vocal and persistent belief that we are made right with God, not by being a part of a covenant community that enjoys God's abundant mercies, but by doing what the law of Moses and the traditions of men demand. The point of the apostolic gospel is that salvation comes through Christ alone, requires only faith in Christ and gives all the glory to God. Anything which extends the boundaries of the means of salvation beyond the person and work of Christ, presenting conditions to be fulfilled by us for God in addition to those that are fulfilled by Christ for us, is a form of legalism.

Nor should the Judaizers be confused with the first-cent-ury Jewish community, because the Judaizers are more closely identified by Paul as being Christians who had combined Christ and the law, particularly Jewish customs concerning circumcision, holy days and food. It's doubtful that they were an organised group coming from one place (the church in Jerusalem) with one or two inspirational leaders (Peter and James). The wedge that was driven by some scholars between Paul the apostle to the gentiles and Peter the leader of the church in Jerusalem is an erroneous one; and the letters that deal with opposition to the gospel suggest much more localised and varied characters.

It is this combination that lies at the heart of Judaizing and legalism. It's the notion that we need the work of the grace of God *plus* a bit of those works of law that we can do, that is the principal, defining feature of the false gospel. The keeping of rules concerning circumcision, days and food was being pressed upon believers then as being essential for a sinner to be justified before God and by God. Nowadays it might be a different set of rules, but the perversion of the content of the gospel, so that it becomes a different gospel that is really no gospel at all, is just the same. It's a false gospel, it's bad news, because at whatever point we bring our bit to our salvation, in order to make up what was supposed to be lacking in God's work, we bring works that are riddled with our sin. The impurity of our motives (doing it just for myself rather than for the glory of God – for personal insurance purposes), or the inadequacy of our repentance (did I forget something? Did I repent well enough?) cast damning shadows over our supposed contribution to our salvation. How could we complement the perfection of what God does by wheeling in our own woefully imperfect additions? It's bad news because it sets us on an awful and endlessly turning treadmill: trying to do enough and trying to do it well enough for a God whose holiness, as we've seen, is way beyond our reach. There is no good news in a gospel that casts me back upon myself for salvation.

False Gospel? Diminished Life!

But there is another sense in which it's bad news, a sense often underestimated but which we highlight here by way of redressing the balance. It's bad news because of the impact on the Christian life. The implications of the false gospel range much wider than the moment when a person becomes a Christian, having heard it preached. The gospel isn't simply the message that brings new life, it's the truth that defines the new life for ever. You can regress into legalism after you've been saved because of a re-working of the gospel. We need to go back to Galatia to see this.

Two ways of living

Paul takes the fight to the Judaizers in the Galatian churches to rescue all believers from a legalistic life: to haul them out of the world of the law into which they are sliding, and back into the world of grace.

How does he do it? Throughout the letter he presents the Galatians (and us, of course) with several contrasts between two ways of living the Christian life. They define for us the falsity of legalism. The first contrast is in the terms that we've been looking at already. We can live according to the different gospel (1:6,7) or we can live according to the apostolic gospel that Paul had preached as he planted churches and to which these Galatians had responded (1:11).

Second, we can live by faith (2:16) or by trying to observe the law (3:10ff); a futile attempt – no-one will escape the curse of the law since no-one will continually do everything in the law. Anyway, God has already laid it down that the righteous will live (not just come alive, note, but live continuously) by faith. The falsity of legalism's 'different' gospel is that it won't work!

Third, we can live according to the promise that God has given – initially in the covenant with Abraham – or we can try to live (*really* live) according to the law: promised gift versus earned reward (3:16ff).

Fourth, we can live the life of a child, enslaved under the governance of the law (3:23ff) or we can live the life of the grown-up heir who has received the full rights of a son (4:4ff).

Fifth, we can live on one of two contrasting lines of spiritual genealogy (4:21ff). The wrong line is that of Abraham's slave Hagar. This line goes through a child born 'the ordinary way' to Sinai and the Mosaic covenant; it leads on to the earthly Jerusalem, which was the power-base of Judaism. This line is about slavery, legalistic living (the law of Moses misused) and being spiritually earth-bound.

The right line, *de facto* the one that has been established and that these Christians are actually on, is the Sarah line; Sarah the free woman, Sarah whose child Isaac was a child born extraordinarily, born of the promise of God believed in by faith (eventually). This line leads to the Jerusalem that is above. This line is about freedom and faith, the promise and a heavenly city. Christians are like Isaac, children of promise and freedom. Note that Hagar was always meant to be Sarah's maidservant – the law was always meant to serve the people of God, not the other way around.

Sixth, we can live according to the Spirit or we can live according to the sinful nature, the flesh (5:16ff) – the Spirit's regenerating work or your own attempted self-regeneration; the Spirit's power or your own.

Paul really hates legalism. By these six recurring and, to some degree interwoven contrasts, Paul demonstrates the falsity of the non-gospel and demolishes the legalist's message. But he has more to say. He sees what kind of quality of life the legalists have produced. He sees two particular ways in which damage has been done to the well-being of the church.

The joyless life

The Galatians are being dragged into a joyless life. Out of genuine and acute pastoral distress, Paul is concerned to make clear to them that their emotional, psychological and spiritual well-being are at stake. It's not merely that their doctrine is being distorted, it's that *they* are being distorted too. 'What has happened to all your joy?' he cries in 4:15. The light of God's joy had been snuffed out as the deadly gas of legalism crept over them. Legalistic fellowships are the most joyless places on earth. But note that it's not simply that they have lost a general ability to experience joy, in itself enough evidence that the Spirit is not at work since joy is part of the fruit of the Spirit in 5:22. What they have lost was the joy with which they had received the word of God. Once, God's word came to them and produced waves of joy in their souls. It was a delight to them. The message put smiles on their faces and a spring in their step. But now, it is was a heavy weight upon their shoulders (5:1).

How true the scriptures are. In legalistic fellowships the word of God brings no joy, it simply burdens us even more. The passages that are preached on all end, one way or another, telling us that we're not doing enough, we're not very good Christians, we're making a mess of it, we don't care about the lost, God isn't very pleased with us. He might love us but he almost certainly finds little in us to like! It doesn't matter where the passage comes from, it always says the same. The letter kills. Another thrashing from the minister! Another subtle beating up from the elders! I've failed again. Life entangled with legalistic laws is a burdensome life.

A loveless church

No surprise then, that the fellowship was now characterised by a lack of love as well as a lack of joy. The attempt at living under the law of Moses had robbed them of yet another segment of the fruit of the Spirit. Instead of recalling and living under the summary of the law that Jesus had recovered from Leviticus (that one commandment: love your neighbour as yourself – 5:14) they had – satanic irony coming up here! – gone for a wrong reading of the law. The very thing that they had chosen to live under should itself (as Paul had pointed out in 3:24) have pointed to a life of love. But instead of protecting one another and serving one another in love, they were 'biting one and devouring each other'. What kind of thing does that phrase mean? It means that they were inflicting injuries by savage words; they were sarcastic. By criticisms and complaints they were using up each other's stores of kindness or patience, instead of building one another up. They were making the Christian life more difficult than it should be. They were doing the work of Satan, who seeks whom he may devour. Their new-found false gospel was taking them down the path of mutually assured destruction. Legalism had hardened their hearts and made them callous. There was no love.

The well-being of your church counts

The emotional, psychological and spiritual well-being of our fellowships is important to God. This is not to condone or encourage a self-absorbed version of Christianity which wants only a God who is nice, who exists only to pander to our self-indulgent whims. But we ought to recognise that, loving us, God is vitally concerned for our well-being. He has saved us for a life of shalom, of complete well-being. If I, being an earthly father, am bothered about my children's emotional condition, how much more is God bothered about ours? If one of my girls comes home from school looking miserable, I want to know what's the matter and I want to try and fix it. If I see my son being stroppy, I don't simply want to stop the bad behaviour that goes along with a strop, I'm also deeply concerned to find out what's got under his skin and bothered him so much.

To an infinitely greater degree, God is concerned about how we feel. Again, let me state that we can't produce an image of God that is purely 'emotionalist': a God whose prime concern is for our emotions, who simply wants us to be happy smiley people all the time and who wouldn't do anything to upset us. His concerns for us run much deeper than that kind of teaching allows. But having said that, we cannot allow the rationalists to rule the roost either. For God made our emotions and made them for his glory. He made us in his image, with something like the emotional range that he demonstrates in the Scriptures. How many of those segments of the fruit of the Spirit that we find in Galatians 5:22 and 23 function at an emotional level as well as in our actions? All of them. Our joy is important to him. Whether or not love springs from our hearts is important to him.

There's more. The state of the Christian and the spiritual climate of the fellowship, shown to a greater degree than we might think by our emotional and relational 'tone', reflects well or badly on the gospel that we preach. Our church 'body language' is crucial. Miserable and loveless Christian fellowships don't sound too convincing when they talk about the joy or the love of the Lord. It's like the proverbial bald man selling hair restorer! Such fellowships don't buttress the truth; their life shouts too loudly for the word to be heard. It is more than a little counter-productive to model the Christian life – however unwittingly and albeit in the name of holiness – as an endlessly uphill struggle against new and tightly controlled social expectations, as a life which always fails to jump a bar that is constantly being raised. The gospel becomes the raised fist against the sinner: a sentence to, rather than salvation from a life of guilt. It's about as winsome as a kick in the teeth.

As a gospel, legalistic Christianity is a deadly and false thing which, more awful than all the other defects of a false gospel, dishonours the one whose glory lies in the gospel. In misrepresenting the God of grace it reeks of hell. In echoing the perverse twisting of what God had said in the garden, it sounds again the subtle hissing of the fork-tongued serpent. In its corruption of the gospel's content and fruit, in its deceptions about the glory of God, it is nothing other than sin. Like Paul, we ought to hate legalism.

5

... Meets the Wonders of God's Grace

Last year I was in hospital. I was nearly sent to heaven by Peritonitis, the Greek god of abdominal infection. During the latter part of my treatment, when I had re-entered the earth's atmosphere, I was on a mixture of antibiotics. Together, they produced a combined effect that brought recovery much more quickly and assuredly than any one of them could have done alone. God's cures for legalism need to work together. To those remedies that can come to us by seeing the truth of sin and the awesome holiness of God, we add the remedy for the false gospel: we open up the wonders of God's grace.

Grace saves the sinner and grace keeps the sinner saved. Grace makes us holy and grace brings us to glory. Even as I write the word ' grace' the sun comes out in my own soul. Writing about the world of legalism is really hard. It means being immersed back in the world that once I knew from the inside. I had forgotten how all-permeating legalism's smog is – it becomes the air that some fellowships and Christians breathe, it gets in the clothes and the furniture, stains the décor, clouds every horizon, sits in the lungs like death. It doesn't matter whether you're in a church service, on a mission, having a Christmas party, or planning a programme of meetings, at some point or another you speak about folk in terms that suggest their unacceptability, and make decisions that reflect your codes of self-justifying conduct. 'Oh, we couldn't ask her to speak, she's a working Mum … I don't think he should be doing the reading he's wearing an ear-ring … I'm not doing the Grand Old Duke of York with *him* – he hardly ever comes to the evening service.' In some way or another legalism always manages to stain life.

On feeling God's Grace

Delight

I want to look at some of the majestically glorious ways of God's grace in a moment – how his grace cures legalism's disease as we are grasped by its wonders: the Spirit's gracious regenerating act, Christ's act of grace in justifying us from all sin, the gracious work of God in sanctifying us and what it means to be in Christ. But for now it's not so much the doctrines that I have in mind, but the effect within us – even upon our emotions – that I'm thinking of.

Receiving and living in God's grace is like the warmth of the life-giving sun; like the sparkling exhilaration of the vast ocean, wave-breaking its delight over the laughing child. Grace is a deep well of sanity and peace; it brings a resting, satisfied calm of perfect contentment. If one glimpse of the holiness of God can cure us of our self-trust, shouldn't it be that one moment in the world of grace should forever ruin us for the world of law? Doesn't even the sound of the word in your heart silence the legalistic whispers, the proscriptive voices of command and control, the demands and manipulative pressures, the sombre disapprovals of the accountants of righteousness? What hope has legalism's whine before the booming glory of the grace of God? Sinfulness has little or nothing to fear from our legalism: the legalism is itself a part of that sinfulness. But sinfulness has no hope before the tidal wave of God's grace.

Grace is so alien to our way of thinking and feeling that it's no surprise that we enjoy it less than we should. Yet its effect upon us, mentally and emotionally, can be greater than we allow it to be, notwithstanding our varied temperaments and cultural backgrounds. We rush, and in the busyness of our Christian lives we miss the benefits of relaxing into the forgiveness and hope that God in his grace has given us in Christ. It takes time to savour the grace of God. We rationalise, but we can love our correct propositions, which we ought to love, so much that we devalue the other sides of our personalities that are just as much made for God. For so many of us feeling the truth – not deciding on truthfulness by our feelings, but feeling the truth – is an art that we have not so much lost as never had. Grace must touch and transform our emotions, but where did those emotions go in our often frantically busy and fearful legalistic Christian lives?

'Glum' is not godly

In many of our churches we have created a glum version of godliness that puts on a morosely weighty mask. But to do what? Fool God? When did you last laugh in prayer, fully relaxed in the presence of the Almighty God who is also your Father, enjoying the joke? Grace lets you do that. Surely you believe that you're going to laugh in heaven? We fix and programme our responsiveness to God and lose the spontaneous delight that properly belongs to being childlike with God. One of the delights of love is that it can take you by surprise and in so doing put a smile on your face that lasts the whole day – well, at least ten minutes if you're busy! But we so regulate our responsiveness to God that we deny him the possibility of taking us by surprise and delighting us with his love. When did you last delight in the creative touches of God's love in a normal day?

'Balanced' is not godly

We qualify our songs and statements to exclude any danger of excess. 'Be balanced' we say. But show me the command to be balanced in the Bible. You can't. It isn't there. I've looked! (No, 'let your moderation be known in all things' isn't the same. Moderation is the restraint of appetites that might otherwise allow us to be overwhelmed with sin, not balancing a little bit of this with a little bit of whatever the opposite might be.) How 'balanced' has God been in his grace towards us? How balanced and unexcessive is the Cross? How measured and carefully meted out is the worship of the saints in heaven? It's way over the top – it involves bowing down and prostrating ourselves before God, not sitting neat and motionless in heaven's perfect pews. The whole Christian life is anything but carefully restrained. It's taking up our cross daily; it's being poured out like a drink offering; it's the total response of my whole being – everything that is within me – to God. It's freedom to run and dance and jump and exhilarate and exult in God, instead of being crippled and shrivelled by rebellion against him. He came to give us what? A carefully measured taste of life? Don't try that one with God: he said that he came to give us abundant life! Brim full and then some; the psalmist's cup overflowed! This is the God we come to in Christ; this is the God of abundant grace.

Doesn't it make you want to read Hebrews 12:18-24 to the Pharisees (and to the Pharisee within) and invite them to see the mountain that they really do live on? For

> You have not come to a mountain that can be touched and that is burning with fire; to darkness, gloom and storm; to a trumpet blast or to such a voice speaking words that those who heard it begged that no further word be spoken to them, because they could not bear what was commanded: 'If even an animal touches the mountain, it must be stoned.' The sight was so terrifying

that Moses said, 'I am trembling with fear.' But you have come to Mount Zion, to the heavenly Jerusalem, the city of the living God. You have come to thousands upon thousands of angels in joyful assembly, to the church of the firstborn, whose names are written in heaven. You have come to God, the judge of all men, to the spirits of righteous men made perfect, to Jesus the mediator of a new covenant, and to the sprinkled blood that speaks a better word than the blood of Abel.

Three wonders of God's Grace

The works of God's grace are fountains of delights for us. Doctrines of grace flow as curative waters for infected souls. Three in particular are worth our attention, so that we might drive out legalism with positive rejoicing and might dispel the false gospel with the wonderful truth of the gospel of grace.

Regeneration

Regeneration is the giving, by the Spirit, of the principle of life to those who were dead in their transgressions and sins. It is a wonderfully humbling cure. I wrote earlier that a greater view of sin should convince us of our need of the work of God alone to free us from its captivity. Our struggles are futile – we are not spiritual Houdinis. Nowhere is this more clear than when we consider what makes us alive – and keeps us alive. It never was and never can be rule-keeping. Not even God's law could bring life. As Paul taught the misled Galatian church, it was only ever given to lead us to the one who alone can give life. Before the Spirit worked within us, we had no vitality of ourselves such that God could work upon us with our co-operation. Only the life of God in the soul of man will do. As the church in Ephesus was taught, being a sinner means not that you're spiritually insensitive, it means that you're spiritually dead (Eph. 2:1). Dead means dead, and not just unwell. Along with that death goes total inability, as far as spiritual life is concerned. The corpse cannot raise itself to life, nor respond to the crash team, nor call for help, nor even work out for itself that it's dead!

So rich is the work of God that it takes multiple words in the Greek of the New Testament to convey the doctrine of regeneration, or new birth. The term for regeneration is *palingenesia*, and only occurs twice – Matthew 19:28 (NIV 'renewal' – the final renewal of all things) and Titus 3:5 ('rebirth' in the NIV, which refers to the believer now). The other terms are *gennao* ('to give birth to', if you're a woman, 'to beget' if you're a man); *apokueo* (which means the same); *ktisis* (which means 'to create'); and *suzoopoieo* ('to make alive with').

In the Old Testament you'll not find many verses that use a word to mean 'born again' but you will find teaching which has a crucial role in shaping the use of the phrase in the New Testament. One passage in particular concerns the regeneration of Israel. Through his prophet Ezekiel, God speaks to his people. They are far from him, loveless and cold towards him, disobedient and unfaithful to the covenant, lifeless and spiritually dead. They have a heart of stone. But God is faithful, full of grace and able to enliven. He comes to them not with fresh laws that they could obey and so, by a supreme dint of law-keeping, perform a self-resurrection. He comes to them instead with a promise of a spiritual transplant, a new heart for a new and faithful life: he says that they will be made spiritually alive.

> I will sprinkle clean water on you, and you will be clean; I will cleanse you from all your impurities and from all your idols. I will give you a new heart and put a new spirit in you; I will remove from you your heart of stone and give you a heart of flesh. And I will put my Spirit in you and move you to follow my decrees and be careful to keep my laws. You will live in the land I gave your forefathers; you will be my people, and I will be your God (Ezek. 36:25-28).

It's after that we are taken to the valley of the dry bones for a dramatised parable, in the introduction to which God says to Ezekiel,

> 'Prophesy to these bones and say to them, 'Dry bones, hear the word of the LORD! This is what the Sovereign LORD says to these bones: I will make breath enter you, and you will come to life. I will attach tendons to you and make flesh come upon you and cover you with skin; I will put breath in you, and you will come to life. Then you will know that I am the LORD' (Ezek. 37:4-6).

Picture the scene ... (I know it's not perfect, but ...)

The victim collapses to the ground. She has been poisoned – bad heroin. Her last moments were ghastly and messy. She lies dead in her filth. Her fall is observed by a man across the street, who rushes to her aid. He knows her, though she has long forgotten him. Anyone seeing the two of them together would perhaps detect, in the right light, a passing resemblance. She is in fact his estranged daughter. Long ago she cut the ties and ran away. For many years he has trailed her. All the privileges of being the daughter of this eminent medical man have been deliberately traded for alienation, fraught with rebellion and enmity. Now she has lost her life.

He must act quickly. He knows well that reviving what's there won't work: nothing less than a transplant will do. Her heart is wrecked. He makes two phone-calls, he picks her up and runs. Crashing through the doors of the hospital he yells commands left and right. He is the consultant cardiologist (you'd guessed that already, hadn't you?) As the staff jump, a police car races up to the doors of A&E with a donor heart. Time is running out, seconds tick her chances away. The team gathers around the body and starts to work on her. The surgeon's skill is guided by his love for his daughter. He takes out the useless mass of damaged muscle that could never be revived and places into the cavity the new heart. It starts, her blood flows, she is given breath, her system is cleaned out. She lives again and learns again to cry out 'Dad!'

Regeneration is necessary for all the other aspects of our redemption. Without it no-one can see the Kingdom of God (Jn. 3:3). It is an instantaneous, internal and once-for-all work of God alone within the individual. As only God created life in Genesis, so only he can implant new life in the re-genesis. It is a work of his 'prevenient' grace, as the boffins call it: grace that comes before any ability on our part to respond. In it the sinner is as totally passive as the dry bones. It is done 'from above' by the Father (see Jas. 1:17-18); with the agency of the Spirit (Jn. 3:8); based upon the resurrection of the Son (1Pet. 1:3); through his word (1Pet. 1:23,25). It results in responsiveness to God's call, faith and repentance, and the start of a new life in Christ which is characterised by Christ-likeness.

All this teaches us the absolute inability of legalism to bring new life and the absolute ability of God in his sheer grace to do just that. Thus far we are following a parallel to the line of argument that Paul uses against legalism when he fires at the Galatians the rhetorical question 'I would like to learn just one thing from you: Did you receive the Spirit by observing the law, or by believing what you heard?' (Gal. 3:2). But the mistake would be to limit the principles in the doctrine of regeneration to the start of the new life. In the next verse Paul goes on to ask 'Are you so foolish? After beginning with the Spirit, are you now trying to attain your goal by human effort?' The mistake of the legalistic mind is to restrict the giving of life to our new birth. The doctrine of regeneration certainly focuses on that, but the life we are given is only, and is for ever, God's life. We aren't jump-started by the Spirit and then left to ourselves to keep life going and to carry on the whole enterprise with some kind of self-perpetuated life of our own. Christ is our life (Col. 3:4). It's the difference between jump-starting a stopped heart and getting a heart transplant.

What a burden is placed upon believers when the Christian

life is presented as the task of keeping oneself alive by keeping the house rules. Of course, as we've noted and need to keep reminding ourselves lest we think this to be someone else's problem, the 'house' can be the most stodgily conservative evangelical or the most far-out charismatic. The rules will be different, but the mentality and the burden are exactly the same. Yet what glorious liberty can be enjoyed when we rest by faith in the truth that our life is in fact the life of the risen Christ, mediated to us by the Spirit. Can we add to Christ's life by either dressing up for church or dressing down, to take a previous example? Is the life of the Son of God deficient, so as to cause us a some shortfall in our life that can only be made up by saying (or not saying) 'Praise the Lord' at the right time? What on earth does legalism hope to add to the resurrection life of God?

How do we apply this cure? It's straightforward but time-consuming; it involves the self-discipline of taking our minds in hand. We will need to re-educate our wills, ambitions and values. It will involve what we'll come back to under the heading of sanctification. It is simple but not easy. 'Since, then, you have been raised with Christ, set your hearts on things above, where Christ is seated at the right hand of God. Set your minds on things above, not on earthly things. For you died, and your life is now hidden with Christ in God' (Col. 3:1-3).

Justification

The next wonder of grace helps us fight the infection of legalism yet more. The inward work of God's grace in regeneration is matched by what is sometimes called his 'external' act of justification – 'external' in that it happens to us but quite outside us. We do not contribute to it at all.

However much our flesh might want to have the satisfaction of doing something to justify itself, and however much our view of the conversion experience might make us emphasise

the importance of our decision, justification is something done
by God for us but without our aid. It is a declaration by God,
on the basis of the cross, that we are clear of all the charges and
all the consequent condemnation that the law could impose
upon us. It is done once and for all – no accusation will ever
separate me from God! All the sins that I will yet commit were
carried then on the cross. It is done by the Father through the
blood of the Son. Put negatively, it means that your guilt and
condemnation are gone (Rom. 8:1). Put positively, you are
restored to your proper family relation with God and all its
many blessings – peace with God (Rom. 5:1); salvation from
death (Rom. 5:9,10); receiving the Spirit (as we saw in Gal.
3:1ff); adoption/sonship, (Gal. 4:4-6 again); the inheritance,
which is eternal life (Tit. 3:7).

Some details about the Bible's words can help us here. In
the Old Testament *tsadaq* (with its variations) is primarily a
legal term that means to be in a right condition as far as the
law is concerned. Thus the word is used in connection with
legal matters in, for instance, Exodus 23:7; Deuteronomy 25:1;
and Isaiah 5:23. You can be in this right condition with
respect to the law either by never breaking the law or by being
acquitted – you can be acquitted either by having the charge
dropped or by paying the price that the law demands. Since
God's law is an expression of his own holy character, being
wrong as far as the law is concerned is to be in a wrong condition before God.

In the New Testament the Greek word *dikaio-o* (and all its
various forms) means the same as the Hebrew *tsadaq* in the Old
Testament. It's a legal term, which Paul employs to describe the
condition in which we are acceptable before God. Thus, for
instance, Romans 8:33. 'Who will bring any charge against
those whom God has chosen? It is God who justifies.' So in the
courtroom the prosecutor and the defendant stand before
the Judge. The prosecution makes a charge and invokes the relevant law. The defendant puts his case – he has basically three

choices: outright denial, mitigating circumstances or wrongful interpretation of the law which has been invoked. The Judge reaches a verdict, finding in favour of the defendant and thus acquits, or 'justifies' him, declaring him to be 'righteous'.

What the New Testament makes clear is that we cannot justify ourselves before God. We have broken his law, so it cannot be the means by which we make ourselves right with God. The law stands against us, condemning us. Thus we have Romans 3:20 that we quoted earlier 'Therefore no-one will be declared righteous in his sight by observing the law; rather, through the law we become conscious of sin.' We can only be justified by the Judge. In this sense it is an 'external' act of God's grace. But on what basis can a holy God acquit us of breaking his own law? He cannot deny the truth of our sinfulness, however much we might like to! There are no mitigating circumstances: we sin! The law is properly invoked and is a just law. The only way for us to be made right with God is for someone else to do two things: to take the punishment that the law demands, thus satisfying it by his vicarious death, and to give us his righteousness by his vicarious life. Both are required for right living with God. Who could do this but the righteous one, Jesus Christ?

Picture the courtroom ...

The defendant is the sinner; me, you. The prosecutor is God's Law. The Judge is God. Christ stands in the dock instead of me. The charges concerning my behaviour are applied to him. The Law is invoked and applied. Judgement is made (guilty). Sentence is passed (you shall die) and carried out (the Cross). The punishment is suffered and the law is satisfied (he dies for me). I am acquitted of all the charges (justified). I hear the good news of this in the gospel and accept it by faith alone (faith is the hearing ear, the seeing eye, the believing heart, with ear, eye and heart enlivened to reach out by the Spirit's work of regeneration). Trusting in Christ's merits and the Father's satisfaction in those merits, I go free: free from the courtroom, free from the burden of the law, and free to live in a proper condition before God

If I can mix the theological terms a bit, we have been given a covering from the terrors of the law – the covering of Christ's blood. Why live as if it were too small a covering? Why stitch onto it with legalistic needlework a few rags of your own right-eousness? Why do we do this in our churches? Are we not mad ('O foolish Galatians, who has *bewitched* you?') But are we not also ungrateful? Isn't it a monumental insult to Christ? And doesn't it call into question the Father's just and eternally valid declaration of justification? The legalist lives as if God were too lenient, merely turning a blind eye to offences that still needed to be dealt with by us. Legalism calls God's justice into question, as well as his grace. Have none of it! Christ's work is enough for the Father to declare you as justified in his sight. He said 'It is accomplished' not 'It is begun.' What an antidote to the spiritual insecurity that legalism creates.

Sanctification

What God has done in regeneration and justification, he brings to our experience in sanctification. Strictly speaking it is not an act but a work – it's on-going, thankfully.

And here the legalists have their firmest foothold. Here our co-operation *is* engaged – we are vitally involved in our increasing Christ-likeness. We worship him with our renewed wills by surrendering them to his will. Whilst on the one hand we are in the position of being holy because we are in Christ, who is our righteousness, holiness and redemption, on the other hand we still don't practice holiness – well, not for very long without a break! So how about a bunch of rules to help us and God along a bit? Well, it certainly seems like a reasonable idea, and it certainly seems a whole lot better than not bothering about holiness, which is what every legalist suspects this book is encouraging!

But to resort to our rule books in order to help God along is, as Paul almost put it, to 'lose the head':

Therefore do not let anyone judge you by what you eat or drink, or with regard to a religious festival, a New Moon celebration or a Sabbath day. These are a shadow of the things that were to come; the reality, however, is found in Christ. Do not let anyone who delights in false humility and the worship of angels disqualify you for the prize. Such a person goes into great detail about what he has seen, and his unspiritual mind puffs him up with idle notions. He has lost connection with the Head, from whom the whole body, supported and held together by its ligaments and sinews, grows as God causes it to grow (Col. 2:16-19).

More detail again ... in the Old Testament the Hebrew *kadash* means 'to sanctify', 'to make holy' or 'to set apart for God'. The tabernacle, altar, priests, etc., were set apart and sanctified for the worship and sacrifice (Lev. 8:10-12). A day could be 'sanctified', set apart for fasting and prayer (Joel 1:14); the Sabbath was holy in this way (Deut. 5:12). The people also were to be holy, even as God himself is holy. Being holy was not primarily as an outward thing that had to do with appropriate ceremonies, though the visible life was involved, but a moral thing that concerned God and sin.

In the New Testament the Greek *hagiazo* (e.g. Mt. 22:17,19) means the same, to set apart, but with the last application prominent. Thus, as the old Smith's Bible Dictionary says, it primarily refers to

the making truly and perfectly holy what was before defiled and sinful, and is a progressive work of divine grace upon the soul regenerated by the Spirit and justified by the love of Christ. After a gradual cleansing from sin the sinner is presented in glory 'unspotted before the throne of God' which is the work of the Holy Spirit (John 14:26; 17:17). The ultimate sanctification of every believer in Christ is a covenant of mercy, purchased on the cross.

I selected Smith's definition because he helpfully puts God's sanctifying grace in the context of the two acts of grace that we've looked at so far: regeneration and justification.

Justification involves the imputing of Christ's righteousness to us. Sanctification involves the imparting of his holiness to us. The difference is between inheriting a sum of money so that it's made over to your name, and using it so that it becomes part and parcel of your life. There are thus some other major differences between the two. Justification concerns our external standing, sanctification concerns our inward condition. We are justified once and for all time; we are sanctified continuously through life. The one was completed there and then on Calvary; the other will be completed there and then in heaven. In justification, no part is played by us; but in sanctification we co-operate. All are justified freely by God's grace to the same degree; some are more sanctified than others. The former is primarily the work of the Father and the Son; the latter is primarily the work of the Spirit and the Son.

But there is also a major and foundational similarity. The Christian is both justified and sanctified in Christ by virtue of union with him in his death and resurrection. Hence Paul can write of our sanctification as being accomplished, while it still needs to be completed: it is, in the tongue of the sages, both positional and progressive. We have it in him, in the sense that Christ is our holiness and his is a perfect holiness, not an increasing holiness. It is imparted gradually to us over time, yes; but what is not yet fully imparted is already all there in Christ. Which in turn means that since his is the only holiness that there is, our increasing holiness can be referred to as increasing Christ-likeness – have a look at 2 Corinthians 3:18 and Ephesians 4:24.

Both are connected with regeneration – justification because the faith that lays hold is ours by gift of new life; sanctification by virtue of the continuance of the new life that the Spirit implants in regeneration. Thus regeneration can be spoken of as sanctification – not complete of course, but assuredly begun (see 1 Cor. 6:11).

Archibald A. Hodge wrote about how sanctification feels. It's in the old speech, but it's no less powerful for that. You can find it in his *Outlines of Theology*:

> The more holy a man is, the more humble, self-renouncing, self-abhorring, and the more sensitive to every sin he becomes, and the more closely he clings to Christ. The moral imperfections which cling to him he feels to be sins, which he laments and strives to overcome. Believers find that their life is a constant warfare, and they need to take the kingdom of heaven by storm, and watch while they pray. They are subject to the constant chastisement of their Father's loving hand, which is only designed to correct their imperfections and to confirm their graces. And it has been notoriously the fact that the best Christians have been those who have been the least prone to claim the attainment of perfection for themselves.

There's not much there about making yourself righteous, but there's plenty about clinging to Christ alone.

In this lies part of the cure for the legalistic, self-sanctifying tendency to which any of us can be prone. Our holiness is holiness with reference to him alone, and it is sourced in the Holy One and in him alone. This brings us freedom from a legalistic holiness which is holy with reference to a Christian social setting, and is sourced in a Christian social setting. Legalism defines our holiness with reference to standards of conduct set within a particular social group. We lose sight of that too easily, ending up with a notion of holiness that is earth-bound and parochial. So we question the sanctity of Luther because he enjoyed beer! Or Calvin because he played bowls on a Sunday. Or Gertrude over there because she let her daughter wear two earrings in the same ear; or Norbert over there who doesn't always seem joyfully victorious in his Christian walk and didn't go on a mission this summer; or Ralph who smokes a pipe. But holiness is bigger than our local boundaries can encompass. Sanctification always takes us back to how we are doing with God and not with the tribe. The transforming progress of Christ's likeness through our whole being makes us holy wherever we are and whoever we are with. So we can be holy with two earrings in Inverness and we can be holy with none in Nairobi. We can be holy with a beer glass in Aberdeen or unholy with a beer glass in Munich. We can be holy at work and at church. We can move with ease and poise between extremes of circumstances, cultures and customs and be uncompromised as regards our holiness before God.

Does that sound dodgy? But Jesus did exactly that: he taught in the synagogue and he feasted at Levi's house. It was the legalists who carped at him and questioned him. He sat and ate with tax collectors and sinners without any of them compromising his holiness. God's work of sanctification enlarges the horizons of the heart; legalism narrows them. God makes us more use in the world; legalism make us less use. God gives us real holiness; legalism gives us a mask that we dare not let the world pull off. God gives us robust holiness; legalism gives us a brittle and fragile parody. And where legalism leaves us incomplete and fearful of meeting God, real sanctification leaves us peaceful and looking forward to the day.

The gift of faith

One final comment, disproportionately significant for its length. The title of this book is *Grace, Faith and Glory*. The grace is God's, so is the glory, as we'll see. The faith is ours. But faith too is a gift from God. It is part of the fruit – the evidence and effect – of the Spirit in our lives, yet we can speak as if it were a work of the flesh and so bring it under our dominion and make it a cause of despair, pride, hypocritical boasting or mask-wearing. In Galatians it is set over against our works. It belongs to the good side along with such terms as 'gospel' 'promise', 'the Spirit' and 'grace', rather than on the bad side with 'flesh', 'works of the law' etc.

Why do I mention this? Why is it essential that we discipline our minds and hearts – which always want to claim some credit – to see faith as a gift? Because otherwise we turn grace into something that we've earned by our faith. Now undoubtedly grace comes to us by means: there are things that we can and must do to lay hold of God's grace and to enjoy it. But these things – which include believing – are not credits that we can build up, like supermarket loyalty card points, in order to buy a fresh bagful of grace. If we turn the wonders of God's grace into God just giving us what we've managed to deserve, then grace is not grace and the wonders are not wonders. Grace is not justice, however just it might be. It is pure gift. Faith is not a meritorious work. It too is a gift. A gift comes from someone else, and you cannot buy it or it is no longer a gift.

Grace, felt and understood and felt yet more, grace laid hold of by faith 'which is the gift of God', this wonderful grace will release the soul from legalism's dead hand.

So what must I do? The simple command

Many of the cures for legalism are aspects of what God has revealed in the Bible which need to be seen, understood and assimilated, then worked out in practice under the Spirit's tutelage. They yield things to do and undo, but in themselves they are facets of truth to understand and absorb. This is part of the process that Paul described when he wrote in Romans 12:2 about being 'transformed by the renewing of your minds'.

But there is something quite specific to do which the truth of God's grace prompts: it's in the Scriptures not as doctrine, but as command. It doesn't sound nice, and I include it with the caveat that for many of us legalism is a matter of being more sinned against than sinning. We've suffered at other people's hands, more than we've been legalistic ourselves. Despite that, there's something of the yearning to justify oneself and trust oneself that is in all of us. We are all as capable of being legalistic as the saints in Galatia were. Recognising a problem might help you against it, but it doesn't mean that you are immune to it. There's something which grace should make us do about our own legalism.

We have to repent.

That about sums it up really. Though perhaps not quite ...

The U-turn

The word is very easy: we make a turn-around in our practices and convictions because of a U-turn in our minds. Both the Hebrew *shuwb* and the Greek *metanoia* mean a turning around, usually turning away from to sin and turning to righteousness and God. In the garden Adam and Eve turned away from God and faced another. They began to reflect not the glory of the One who had made them but the coiled up twistedness of the one who had deceived them. Repenting means turning so that once again we face our Maker, but now we face him who has become our Redeemer also. In fact, the Hebrew has a strong flavour of returning, turning back to a path once walked but now departed from. Take as an example the words of Solomon as he prayed at the dedication of the temple in Jerusalem – foreshadowing in that earthly copy the real temple that is above, to which we turn in repentance and cry out for mercy. He speaks of his errant fellow-Israelites and knows both the word of God and the faithfulness of God to his word. Clearly he has those defining chapters Deuteronomy 28 to 30 in mind, anticipating, as God does in Deuteronomy, that they would sin against God and be sent into captivity. Solomon prays:

> If they have a *change of heart* in the land where they are held captive, and *repent* and plead with you in the land of their conquerors

and say, 'We have sinned, we have done wrong, we have acted
wickedly'; and if [that is] they *turn back* to you with all their heart
and soul in the land of their enemies who took them captive, and
pray to you towards the land you gave their fathers, towards the
city you have chosen and the temple I have built for your Name;
then from heaven, your dwelling-place, hear their prayer and their
plea, and uphold their cause (1 Kgs. 8:47–49).

'Change of heart', 'repent', 'turn back': three parallel descriptions of their transformation and *shuwb* is used for each one.

Put simply, repentance is a Godward about turn on the inside
that transforms our outward behaviour. That inward turn may
involve more or less remorse and more or less of a guilty feeling but you can have these without ever actually repenting.
Repentance goes the whole distance right through to being a
new person before God.

And it is the proper response to God once we become aware
of our own legalism. Before we can remove specks, the plank
must go. Most of us have the propensity for self-justification, for
keeping ourselves acceptable to God, for wresting assurance out
of his hands and attempting to hold it in our own, for self-
cleansing by the works of our laws and the traditions of our
tribe. That weakness compromises our faith. Only partially or
momentarily trusting a righteousness which is from God, we
seek a righteousness which is our own. We try and qualify. It's
not that we should jettison all standards and go for anarchic
antinomianism, it's that our standards of conduct, even God's
standards revealed in Scripture, can become credits that we
notch up. We can all turn the principles for a life of faith lived
in the power of the Spirit, and twist them into the criteria for
a life of qualification lived in the power of our own flesh. When
we spot this in ourselves the cure is repentance. It's a sin: forgiveness is needed. It won't come by us putting on some new
theological kit: it will come as we repent of the rags and tatters
of legalism. Its guilt won't disappear as we fill our minds with

helpful teaching: it will disappear as we are cleansed by the blood of Jesus Christ again and again and again.

From those who suffered most from the search for extreme legal righteousness, and who inflicted most suffering on others, Jesus expected repentance. Quizzed by the chief priests and the elders as he walked in the temple as to the authority by which he spoke (because it wasn't theirs!) Jesus replied with a parable. In Matthew 21:28ff a father asked his two sons to go and work for him in his vineyard, the kingdom. One son says no – the legally inappropriate answer – but then changes his mind and goes. The other says yes – the correct answer – but doesn't actually go. That same change of mind had been shown by those in the crowds that heeded Jesus, even though they had once given every indication of being 'unrighteous'. Despite being sinners, they had believed the message about the Kingdom and the Christ that John had spoken and they had repented.

From the Scribes and Pharisees, however, who had all the correctness, came no repentance. Those who thought themselves right with God were unrighteous; and those who were thought to be the unrighteous had become right with God. 'For John came to you to show you the way of righteousness, and you did not believe him, but the tax collectors and the prostitutes did. And even after you saw this, you did not repent and believe him' (Mt. 21:32). It reiterates what Jesus had said earlier, with such biting irony, to the Pharisees and the teachers of the law, the Scribes. They muttered about him and sneered at him because of the unrighteous, unclean company that he kept. In reply he gave them the three parables about finding the lost sheep, the lost coin and the lost son. 'I tell you that in the same way there will be more rejoicing in heaven over one sinner who repents than over ninety-nine righteous persons who do not need to repent. (Luke 15:7 – you need to put inverted commas round the word righteous to make the point.)

The way to respond to God when your sin becomes apparent is exactly the same whether you're a tax-collector, prostitute or ' sinner' (the three categories of unrighteousness in those two passages) or whether you're a deeply religious, conservative-minded, biblically literalist, highly moral, fully paid-up card-carrying evangelical legalist. The 'upright' legalist is in the same mess as the whore. Salvation from that common mess comes the same way for whoever is in it. Both kinds of people, the 'righteous' and the 'sinner', need real salvation. They both need a work of God that not only brings freedom from sin's author, power, guilt and penalty, but which also brings fresh life, fresh love, fresh blessings from God. 'Repent, then, and turn to God, so that your sins may be wiped out, that times of refreshing may come from the Lord' said Peter in Acts 3:19.

Parched in the arid and joyless desert of your own legalism? Repentance is the way to times of refreshing. Wearied by the treadmill of legalism? Repentance is the way to times of refreshing. Dry-mouthed in your praise through legalism's malaise? Repentance is the way to times of refreshing. And in the face of God's wonderful grace, who would not want to repent?

6

Legalism Robs God

Legalism is useless against sin and it corrupts the gospel that we both preach and live by. These problems contribute to a warping of our faith that finds its worst effects in the way that legalism robs God of his glory. It robs him of his glory in the gospel, as we've already seen, and it robs him of the glory that should be his in the lives of his redeemed and reconciled children. This is legalism's most vile sin. It is this that makes it more than just a problem from which some personality types suffer, more than just a feature of church style and far, far more than any slight defect that might crop up in the fellowship. In this, it rebels against God's great purpose in making and saving us: his glory. It etches disfigurement into the glory of God in the face of Christ. It denies him his glory in his sovereign, redeeming grace and it denies us the God-honouring joy of resting in him alone.

In this chapter I want to lay out more clearly some of the ways that the legalistic life ends up denying God the glory. As before, God has his remedies: they wonderfully liberate us from the false lordship and caging constrictions of legalism and release us into more of the unshackled joy of the Lord.

Faith and 'Un-faith'

God, in his majesty and infinite glory, is glorified by our faith. He who is above the heavens and the earth, is yet exalted higher when we find in him all our hope, all our satisfaction, all our joy and all our sufficiency. By faith we say to him that we are insufficient and that he alone is sufficient to save and to keep us. By trusting in him and not ourselves or any other thing or person that we have selected for the position of a god, we say that he is the glorious one. He not only deserves to be but actually is the sole object of our worship and praise. We praise him by trusting in him alone.

Grace and faith came before the law

Legalism robs God of this exaltation by faith, robs him of the glory that is due to his name. If we can put it in terms of the plan of redemption, by seeking to establish our initial and continuing acceptance with God upon any ground other than his grace-work for us, we invert the historical, biblical pattern of salvation. Before Israel had laws to obey – as we've already noted, 430 years before – God made a covenant of grace with Abraham, restated it with his son-of-faith Isaac, and in turn with his son, Jacob. The relationship between God and his people was established by the promise of God; the sanctions were given by God. Unilaterally, upon his initiative and without any negotiation of terms, an eternal covenant was forged. In it, the just live by faith in the One who forged it. Abraham was justified by his faith, displaying God's way of salvation which still applies to us now. By that covenant and faith Abraham belonged to God and lived 'in the face of God'. So do we. God's sovereign and initial grace, not Abraham's good deeds, was to the glory of God. Abraham, Isaac and Jacob were to obey God's command, yielding to his greater power and authority.

There was behaviour appropriate to belonging to God and worshipping him and there was inappropriate behaviour. God gave the law through Moses on Sinai in order to codify that behaviour, significantly just after the rescue from both the angel of death and the somewhat less angelic death-carrying chariots of Pharaoh. Thus before the law is given God is exalted as Saviour and Victor. This is the first part of the great praise given to God by Moses and all the Israelites after the Red Sea deliverance:

> I will sing to the LORD, for he is highly exalted. The horse and its rider he has hurled into the sea. The LORD is my strength and my song; he has become my salvation. He is my God, and I will praise him, my father's God, and I will exalt him. The LORD is a warrior; the LORD is his name. Pharaoh's chariots and his army he has hurled into the sea. The best of Pharaoh's officers are drowned in the Red Sea. The deep waters have covered them; they sank to the depths like a stone. Your right hand, O LORD, was majestic in power. Your right hand, O LORD, shattered the enemy (Ex. 15:1-6).

Just as significantly, the law was given before entry into the long-promised land. In Canaan they would face the pressures and the temptations of idolatrous living. There, in their own land, they would establish their own laws, customs and traditions in a way which had been impossible in Egypt. There they could honour God by faithful obedience to his word – or they could dishonour him by disobedience. There they could shine as a light to the nations around, demonstrating by their holiness the holiness of Jehovah. In the land they could trust in him and so show the trustworthiness of the living God over against the powerless idols. From there they could expand the sphere of good government and extend the borders of grace to those living in darkness.

The written code framed life in the land for them. It was never intended to bring the dead to life. Only the Spirit of God could do that. It was never meant to cover sin and so save from judgement. Only the blood of the lamb could provide, or perhaps only even signify, such covering. It was never meant as a substitute for faith and obedience. The law was never meant as a definer of who was in and who was out – do this and you'll belong, and belonging you'll be saved: faith was the touchstone of being one of the people and the only way to live with the Holy One. Witness Rahab, for example. Before she'd learned of the ten commandments or ever seen the tabernacle, she had real faith in God, real reverence for his saving power, and her faith showed itself in both her words and her actions. In this salvation which comes by faith, God is glorified. Salvation was complete prior to the law: Abraham was as much God's man as Moses was. It needed no completing by works which the law prescribed. What Jehovah did for man by his grace and promise was all that needed to be done and all that could be done. You might as well try sticking a fancy aerofoil on an eagle as adding to what God had done in order to improve it! So the glory goes to God in his grace.

What he has done in Christ is to fulfil that covenant from both sides: from ours for us, since we are unable to keep our side of it, and from his since he is well able to keep his side of it. So from our human side Christ fulfils the faith and obedience – Christ the true Israel of God, Christ the Proper Man – and from God's side Christ fulfils his saving work – saving us from sin and death, from Satan and Satan's domain. Christ's glory now, as before, lies in his redeeming grace.

Who gets the glory?

By establishing a degree of self-sufficiency in salvation, legalism robs God. By putting law before grace, the code before the covenant, the fruit of righteousness before the gift of righteousness, it robs God. It robs him of the glory of his lordship, his sovereignty in salvation. Some other power is needed, some other sceptre needs to extend over sin. We assume a power to save and to keep. Some throne-sharing is called for. It robs him of the glory of his redeeming grace in Christ, the glory of his tender and mercifully patient perseverance with us and the glory of the Spirit's sanctifying power.

By legalism we rob God of his glory and place it upon ourselves. We usurp the Spirit's sole work in bringing the dead to life and thus proclaim our lordship over death. We usurp the Son's sole work in bearing sin and so proclaim our lordship over Satan. We usurp the fountainhead of the Father and become the source of our existence and wisdom. We lay hold of the glory that should go to God.

In so doing, we rob God of that further glory that comes from enjoying him. As John Piper puts it, we glorify God *by* enjoying him for ever. But by our legalism we create a life that cannot feel the joy of the freedom of the children of God. The life created by legalism can never enjoy the peace of finding all its satisfaction in God. Such a life will restlessly seek satisfaction in that which supposedly will add to what God has already done. Profound discontent and dis-ease flow from unbelief in the complete sufficiency of God. Only a dissatisfied life can grow from such soil. And such dissatisfaction with God robs him of his glory. It proclaims that he isn't enough. Never will the legalistic heart enjoy the abandonment of self to God. No wonder that in legalistic fellowships of any ilk the 'worship' can become so stylised and programmatic, so mind-bogglingly lifeless, so contrived and unspeakably predictable. Both Abi and Mark could have written in advance a detailed report of their two very different services. There was little risk of overwhelming joy in God breaking out and changing things. No wonder the legalist's soul never soars with praise in freedom from self-regard. In each of their churches, Abi and Mark knew only too well that when the people sang they usually had only one eye on the Lord. The other was mostly on the rest of the worshippers. No wonder heaven never rings to the songs of the legalist's heart.

By its 'unfaith' in God and by its dissatisfaction with him, legalism attacks the heart of worship. God redeemed us so that we might enjoy by faith the complete sufficiency of his grace, and thereby glorify him. Legalism sucks the life out of such God-honouring enjoyment.

Legalism is boring

Legalism is narrow-minded and sinfully boring.

I need to qualify that immediately. It is absolutely right that we counter any attempt to evaluate the truth or otherwise of a message by criteria that have more to do with entertainment than with the word of God. We live in a world which constantly seeks novelty. The ceaseless search for some new and preferably exciting experience or teaching is a curse upon the church; it comes from a restless and disordered world, not from the Holy Spirit. God is not obliged to provide us with some new gimmick every time we show signs of boredom with life. Neither is he under any contract to permit us to let our minds roam wherever they will – they would wander astray from him and from his truth if he did. Every thought is to be brought captive to Christ. It is a narrow path that leads to eternity: narrow with respect to wilfulness and sin, but not with respect to life.

Our Maker is never boring

Yet God, who brings us into a spacious place and the glorious freedom of a world of grace, is endlessly creative. Each sunset differs from the previous one. Each evening he shifts and flexes light so elusively, that before we know it, the sky is altered. Coastlines transform with tides and seasons; no two stretches are the same. No two snowflakes are identical; as one falls upon your hand it changes and vanishes, thermodynamics of breathtaking complexity and beauty. Our finger-prints and irises are all different. All five billion plus of us. Plants grow in uninhabited deserts for no-one else to see but him – presumably just because he enjoys them. He paints on an infinite canvas. Galaxies abound that only he and the angels see. He creates new stars for the sheer joy of it! He is constant but never static like wallpaper or the pillars of a church. Our God is always moving, always working, ceaselessly creative, dazzlingly original, infinitely imaginative. Never a mere copier, he is the one true genius. In that particular sense he is always fun – dare we use the word in a church that has become afraid of the full reality of a God who, without compromising his holiness, makes the hippopotamus, the ostrich, the chameleon and the goat! He is a God to admire, appreciate and applaud, to laugh with and to wonder at: a God whose continually inventive company is a delight; a God to like. Do you like God? Or have you done the semantic soft-shoe shuffle with God that we do with folk at church: you can love them without actually having to like them? Is the one you serve actually someone that you'd like to spend an evening with?

The boring legalist

Yet under the guise of seriously seeking holiness, legalism makes the narrow path narrower than God made it. God makes the way narrow with respect to sin, because it is his way and he is the antithesis to sin. Out of a fear of transgression that has never been outweighed by faith in the power of God over sin, legalistic fellowships make it narrow with respect to life. And it really doesn't matter what end of whatever church spectrum the fellowship happens to be.

Most of the legalistic fellowships, organisations, groups or individuals that I've had any contact with have been more or less negative, down on fun and narrow: you really want to say to these folk 'Get a life'. For them, God's creation isn't to be enjoyed; much of it is to be avoided, or else it's seen as a light distraction from the really serious matters of so-called theology.

Nature is only interesting as far as has to do with the creation/evolution debate. Music, theatre, cinema, art? Worldly and probably sinful, so best avoid them. Literature, especially poetry, has to be endured if you really must do English at university. (And if you choose to, you place a question-mark over your faith.) You separate yourself from culture in case it stains you. Admittedly, sex was designed by God but its attraction is probably best denied by us on account of it being dirty, apart from the necessities of reproduction. (Though secretly ...) Intelligence and wit are frowned upon (out of envy). Joy is only a sense of relief that you've got the religious task done. Birthday cakes in church? Frivolous soul-candy. Hugs are ... well, ugh! As for holidays!

But it gets much worse – sinners aren't to be loved, they're to be evangelised as an exercise in self-justifying discipleship and beyond that, best avoided lest they stain you too. If you can't have correct evangelistic contact, it's better to have as little as possible. People, in all their complexity and contradictions, aren't to be understood with compassion – they are to be judged and told what to do: the objects not of love, but of expectations.

Sinfully boring

This restricted life, this trussed up, dull and joyless life is boring: seriously, and here's the rub, *sinfully* boring. Why sinfully so? Because it is boring in a way that denies the full range and richness of the humanity that God made and has redeemed. It's sinful because it robs God of the glory that is his in the crown of his creation: in us. We were made to the glory of a never-boring, eternally creative and staggeringly ingenious God; we were redeemed at immeasurable cost for precisely that glory. Every faculty, aptitude, ability and gift is to glorify God. Yet by narrowing life into that limited and hamstrung parody passed off as the Christian life, God is trimmed, lessened. God, who does the best art, the best drama, the best literature, the most refreshing diversions from unremitting toil, the most tactile compassion, the best and most diverse evangelism, the most creative ways to reach complex human beings with his love, this God is not exalted, he is diminished in our eyes and before the world.

And so is our saltiness and our light-bearing. Is it any wonder that we make so little redemptive impact upon the worlds of cinema and literature, the performing and expressive arts in all their diversity, science and technology, philosophy, economics, politics, business and commerce, architecture and planning, trade and academia? We have narrowed the scope of redeemed *life* by our legalism as much as by any other failing. We have omitted to mention the Creator God in the galleries, opera houses and banking halls, in the council chambers and the restaurant kitchens. The scope of redemption becomes narrow, not expansive; the redeemed life becomes boring, not abundant. There is no exultant joy in the legalistic life, in this life of sinful omissions; and in this God is profoundly and wickedly dishonoured.

Damagingly boring

His people are not helped either. It cuts against the grain, this boring minimisation of life. We were made for more than the performance of a controlled and limited set of functions. We were made to honour the One who created us in his image by reflecting that image back to him as well as to the rest of creation. In Christ, we have been re-made so that we might re-image God. The Perfect Man is our new humanity, the image re-borne, restated, repainted. By narrowing down the Christian life we cut against the grain. Counter to his purpose of expanding our humanity from the shrivelled corpse into which sin had turned it, we keep it small and undeveloped.

We do this with at least two disastrous effects.

Marginalisation

In the first place, by narrowing down the Christian life legalism quietly and very effectively marginalises people in our fellowships who don't fit. Their interests, tastes or personalities don't register positively on the collective indicators. For example, the fellowship that quietly and smugly scorns opera as being 'not very spiritual', even 'worldly', will register an enthusiastic opera-lover as spiritually less acceptable. What does that do to the opera-lover? It gives them a choice: to suppress the God-given love of opera and enter the approved circle of approved Christians, or to carry on going to concerts and evening classes and listening to the CDs but be confined to the margins of the fellowship.

The same self-righteous scorn can, and quite commonly does, extend to the world of work: so-called 'secular' employment. It's that which you have to do between the acceptably religious activities, a distraction from the 'spiritual' stuff that goes on at church. But this down-grades 'secular' employment. By this attitude the claim that God is honoured in the day job is regarded with suspicion; a question mark hangs over the claimant's commitment or their growth in the Lord. The legalism kicks in. Forcing a divorce between the self-justifyingly 'sacred' and the dangerous 'secular', the legalistic mind hedges the world around with a dividing barrier of value-laden rules and regulations. By such insinuations and self-righteousness, true holiness is confined to the merely religious activities.

The tendency for legalistic minds to set standards for acceptance applies to personality types as well. There are fellowships that place a spiritual premium on affluence, looking as if you've definitely got life together and are visibly full of confidence. The apparently successful Christian is immediately accepted in a way which is laden with spiritual value-judgements, but which in reality is more to do with purely social criteria. But some people just aren't smiley; they aren't effusively out-going and radiant with confidence. Some people aren't 'successful': they struggle with life, self and God and they look like they're struggling. If they give an honest answer to the question 'How are you?' – an answer that doesn't start with the word 'fine' – then they're obviously not Living in Victory, are clearly Under Oppression and might well have been placed under an Evil Anointing. Or something. They certainly aren't loved by God's people in the unconditional way that God loves them. They become marginalised.

Kept on the fringes, the opera-lover, the Christian in the workplace and the 'failure' are denied the experience of love and the opportunities for service that should be theirs. Many of the blessings that are meant to come as part of the fellowship of believers pass them by. Where do the marginalised enjoy the benefits of supportive prayer in time of need, wise and enlightening counsel about work-issues, compassionate understanding of temptations, spiritually stimulating exchanges about Scripture and life, unconditional acceptance? If they stopped turning up, would it draw a genuinely friendly enquiry? Or would they receive a sternly corrective visit that would simply reinforce their sense of not making the grade? Or would they just not be noticed? They might experience more friendship and fellowship among the non-Christians at work or at the pub than they do at church.

Inducing guilt

In the second place we create that most common of emotions: guilt. How? Part of the dynamic of the law that it awakens in us the desire to sin. Paul writes in Romans 7:7-8 that 'I would not have known what coveting really was if the law had not said, "Do not covet." But sin, seizing the opportunity afforded by the commandment, produced in me every kind of covetous desire.' This is true of God's law in the Old Testament, which is what Paul is talking about, and it's just as true of our additional laws.

What happens when we narrow down the Christian life with restrictions that God has never placed upon it? We encourage an attitude of rebellion. We put up signs that say 'Don't walk on the grass' and what do we accomplish? We encourage experimental grass-walking!

Our false and pseudo-spiritual commandments do the same as God's good law. They give sin in us an opportunity to rebel. Only where God's good laws afford sin the opportunity to lead us into real sins, with a consequent real guilt before God, our legalistically produced traditions afford that same rebellious streak the opportunity to lead us into something that's not really sinful, just labelled as such by us. The consequence is an entirely false guilt. It might be powerful and pervasive but it's a totally unnecessary burden. God, in his grace, invites us to enjoy his rest, for 'his yoke is easy and his burden is light.' But by presenting fresh stimuli to our rule-breaking minds and by inducing so much false guilt, legalism makes that rest more elusive. It leads us away from Christ's promised abundance of life. It sounds a death-knell to the enjoyment of God. We create the uneasy background of guilt that so many Christians live with: assuming that something must be wrong with them when all the time it's something wrong with what's being pressed upon them.

In both these ways, we frustrate the development of Christian character. Cutting against the grain of God's life in our souls, we frustrate his reshaping work. Carving and whittling away at the wood with our own legalistic tools we disfigure the image. By defining life more narrowly than God does and being sinfully boring, legalistic Christianity snuffs out the vitality of life in Christ.

7

Legalism Trivialises Life

There is a distortion of the life of grace, lived by faith to the glory of God which is deeply and bitterly ironic. The mind-set of the legalist has shades and casts of genuine virtue. The Pharisees of Jesus' day are easily and commonly caricatured by us as being completely out of court as far as anything admirable goes: all of them utterly corrupt and vile. Yet it was the Pharisees who were keen to see the law adhered to for the sake of right-eousness. They made a considered and persistent attempt to live holy lives that kept away from sin. They prized the law; their interpretations of it were classically conservative. As Tom Hovestol has demonstrated in his superbly clear and piercingly challenging book *Extreme Righteousness*,[1] we only need to glance at them to see ourselves in them. They were serious people. Not given to a frothy, good-time faith, they took the call to holiness seriously; not just private holiness either, but com-munal holiness. Theirs was no individualistic religion. It is an irony that ought not to pass us by that we find in the Pharisees (and in the scribes, the teachers of the law) such zeal for right-eousness, yet such energetic destruction of the possibility of being really righteous. Their aim of righteousness is ironic,

---

[1] Tom Hovestol, *Extreme Righteousness*, Moody Press, Chicago, 1997

given their methods and their achievements. The irony is a bitter one in that their methods took them so far that they ended up directly contradicting, hating and (via the Sanhedrin) crucifying the Righteous One.

There is another edge to the irony, though, which we might more readily miss. It is connected to the ease with which the keen can be so easily persuaded that the legalistic life is the one to be pursued. For all its seriousness about leading a holy life, legalism then and now trivialises the Christian life. It sounds crazy doesn't it? The legalists that we know find the thought of trivia abhorrent. They seem to be predisposed against a fun-loving, entertainment-seeking view of the Christian life. They commit serious amounts of time to church. They are keener that most on evangelism, they can smell worldliness from a mile away and can identify potential temptation hot-spots in the most innocent of circumstances. Legalism gives top-drawer Christianity a bad name, not the mediocre, compromised stuff. On the surface, legalism is deadly serious.

Legalism's trivial pursuits

Therein lies one of the most bitter ironies of legalism: it fills life with rules that govern non-essentials. In doing so, it not only induces layers of false guilt, as we've seen; it also gives our lives the wrong focus.

Our capacity for inventing new problems that require new rules is almost infinite! The extreme form is a kind of Christian neurosis that manically churns out fresh regulations for the fellowship, or for the self. New criteria for being a good Christian spring forth with an inventiveness that, if used more productively, could transform the global economy, eradicate all major diseases and devise a sensible transport policy for the world's major cities! We are phenomenally clever when it comes to discovering new-fangled teachings in our Bibles that warn against this or that dire consequence of not doing what

someone else says – usually it's the pastor. But we don't even
need the Bible: the essence of the nominal 'churchiness' that
bedevils denominations great and small and which hardly opens
the Bible, is that the proper performance of the formalities fulfils all righteousness. Get the paperwork or the dress code or the
liturgy right and you're okay. Woe betide that son of perdition
who reads from the wrong page in the Service Book.

Does it really matter if your hair is longer than the fellowship regulations? Is that hat virtuous (or sinful, depending on
your fellowship and the hat!)? Is God actually that bothered by
jeans? What if you just don't feel like lifting up your hands on
the third repeat of *Shout to the Lord?* What if you find this or that
style of music attractive – does that make you spiritually sub-
standard, or spiritually upright?

You see the point? Legalism elevates the non-essentials and
so fixes our attention on things that the Bible rates as relatively
unimportant if not downright trivial: on matters of personal
taste and preference, on criteria that reflect nothing more than
our social background and the traditions of our tribe. Legalism
trips us up with pedantries when we should be running and
dancing with joy in God. Under the banner of taking everything seriously, it trivialises life with God.

Pedantic is not the same as godly

The problem becomes acute when we confuse being pedantic
with being godly. How so? It occupies our energies in the tasks
of moral hair-splitting. We strive not to maintain unity but to
maintain our legally defined purity. Our efforts and attention
are taken up with separating ourselves from the impure. So we
pay lip service to being all one in Jesus Christ and then get on
with the supposedly spiritual work of trashing others who read
a different translation of the Bible! This kind of pedantry over
unimportant details reinforces that background level of guilt
that we just mentioned and that no child of God should ever

have to live with. It is not unknown where I live for Christian girls to feel the need to change out of their jeans and put on a skirt when they make the Sunday afternoon phone call to their parents on the Scottish west coast.

Legalism diverts attention away from our primary task on earth: taking the gospel to a sinful world. Secondary to the dictates of self-created righteousness comes the eternal fate of millions, including our neighbours. Splitting hairs with fellow-Christians does much more to bolster the in-turned and insecure legalist's spiritual ego, than can ever be done by reaching out to the man across the street who washes his car on Sunday to the sound of rock music blaring from his teenage son's bedroom.

It teaches all the wrong lessons to our children. It teaches them that to react against the fellowship's constraints is synonymous with reacting against God himself. So when they reach the years when they're supposed to be finding out and establishing who they are, they are dumped with the spiritual charge of being in rebellion. True, they might be fed up with religion and they hanker after a good old sin when the oldies aren't looking or, even more pleasurably, when they are. True, they can find themselves dragged or wilfully running into self-destructive habits that wreck their opportunities, cause untold havoc in the family and wring their parents' hearts with deepest pain. But it's also true that as they pass through the years of chaotic turmoil or of the quiet adoption of an adult persona, the last thing they need to be told is that they can't wear jeans to church, or that they must be able to learn from their minister's preaching style, or else they are backsliding. Backsliding from what? Not from grace nor from righteousness. Cage a child with rule-governed religion and you've lost the teenager. Even if they stay in the cage.

By equating pedantry with godliness we alienate others in our churches. We make (so-called) godliness an impossibility for those who naturally have been given a more laid-back temperament. Don't get me wrong: it's not that being laid-back is inherently virtuous, any more than being rule-dominated is either. It's that we can set up a fellowship, in terms of its psychology and values, to portray godliness as something that's going to be unattainable by some simply because of their God-given temperament and personality. Some people don't function with a set of rule-governed flow charts. They aren't made that way. Their Maker made them easy-going and laid-back. Insist that they please their Maker by trying to be someone that they are not, is like trying to fit a cat into a dog's body – it just won't work and if you try, you'll ruin the cat

Back to Mark from earlier in the book. Mark is congenitally incapable of being punctual. He's never spectacularly late, but he reasons that the two or three minutes by which his punctuality is regularly let down are no more than the collective margin of error in everybody's watches. Who could actually say when 7.30pm really came and went? He also reasons that his two or three minutes don't actually make a scrap of difference to the Spirit's power. He rebukes himself when he knows that he has let people down, but he's just never going to be punctual. He wasn't made that way. Neither was he made to witness by the rule-book, nor to organise every last detail of a home Bible study according to the Pastor's rubric. His flat is not all that tidy and his desk at work looks like the 'after' picture in a demolition firm's brochure. Mark is made to be easy-going, and apart from checking to see if there's any plain old thoughtlessness in his conduct, his godliness simply cannot be measured by his step-by-step conformity to every letter of the house rules.

There has to be an expansiveness in our churches that gives breathing space and elbow room to those whose Creator has made to be 'laid back'. We can't force the Lord's children into clothes that just don't fit. It's of the essence of good teamwork to utilise the temperamental differences between members of the team. Make the team's tasks the object of its focus and you can use distinctiveness successfully; make personality difference the focus and you've lost it. The expansiveness comes, of course, from love. Love accepts others as God has made them. It gives the right-mindedness that doesn't suffer fools gladly yet doesn't label as rebellious subversives those like Mark who don't follow every letter of Church Rule 48, para. 13, subsection d, part ii.

What's the focus of your life?

But more than making us damagingly constrictive or ridiculously pedantic, legalism trivialises life at a far more pernicious level. It shifts the focus of our lives onto a dangerously convincing alternative to God himself. Our focus shifts onto our religion: the Christian 'stuff' that we do. Because it is religious, even in the good sense of the word, it therefore seems to be a valid and important focus for life. But our lives were not made for religion: they were made for God.

Of course, a sentence like that could come from anyone who is fobbing off an invitation to come to church or read the Bible or take part in some other Christian activity ('Oh, I don't need to go to church to worship God – I can be just as near God on the golf course ...') And it could also come from a lukewarm Christian who's justifying a drift away from the fellowship of believers. Yet it can also come from the psalmist. Psalm 63 is stunningly intense. It is a cry from the heart, a cry from the desert. Away from the temple, away from the activities and appearances of religion we hear the deepest longings of the psalmist's heart and soul. Take a man who loves God into the wilderness, strip him of all the religion that could have become the focus of his life, remove the rituals and the regulated, choreographed and highly organised practice, confiscate any crutch, and what do you find? You find what the true focus of his life is. And it is God himself. Maybe it's a focus that can only be created by the privations and starkness of the desert, but not necessarily so: deserts don't automatically produce godliness – those who murmured in the desert during the Exodus longed to go back to Egypt for the cucumbers! It is God who has

always been the psalmist's focus, even during the most religious
moments. So in eleven verses we have no fewer than eighteen
occurrences of 'you' or 'your' with reference to God. With a
power and depth of feeling that even among the psalms is
remarkable, he floods the psalm with longing for God and for
God himself. Shamelessly he opens the depths of his own heart.
Take the first eight verses:

> God, you are my God,
> earnestly I seek you; my soul thirsts for you,
> my body longs for you,
> in a dry and weary land where there is no water.

> I have seen you in the sanctuary
> and beheld your power and your glory.

> Because your love is better than life,
> my lips will glorify you.
> I will praise you as long as I live,
> and in your name I will lift up my hands.

> My soul will be satisfied as with the richest of foods;
> with singing lips my mouth will praise you.

> On my bed I remember you;
> I think of you through the watches of the night.

> Because you are my help,
> I sing in the shadow of your wings.
> My soul clings to you; your right hand upholds me.

It's what the heart of every believer should feel and say; it's the
outpouring of the soul's true love, the revelation of its real pre-
occupation, the mapping of its true territory. It's also an invitation
to the merely religious mind to shift its focus from religion, even

good religion, onto God himself. Even when the psalmist thinks of the sanctuary he longs not for it but for the one he saw there.

God made us to enjoy and glorify him, not to become religious flunkeys. Of course, he gave ways in which to approach him. The religion, which the psalmist sees beyond, is itself God-given. But if we fail to distinguish between God himself and the ways that we worship him, we set ourselves up for the vacuously religious life. With God-directed worship, as with so many of God's other gifts, the lure for hearts that have not yet fixed on him, in fact the lure for the flesh, is to fix onto the gift instead. But of all people, God's redeemed should be the least likely to be duped by the attractions of religious form: we know the power of God himself. This is our great inheritance in Christ: we have him. Who wants the shadows when you can know the real person?

All things were made by God and for him. So God himself – not the things of God but God himself – is the highest, best and true focus of all his creation. In Christ, we have been re-made for him, but when we focus on satisfying the demands of law, our focus is shifted onto something *less* than its true ground and we rob God of the glory of lives that are fully devoted to him. Our motives and preoccupations change – no longer is our chief end to glorify God and enjoy him for ever; instead we do stuff for approval from the controllers or to earn something from God. Having all that we need for life and godliness in Christ means that we are freed from the burden of that kind of life and that we are freed for the genuinely serious yet never glum pursuit of enjoying God himself for himself. Seeking him with all that we need already and assuredly ours in Christ, we are not trapped by seeking merely what we can gain from him. We are able to love him with something more than cupboard love. And thus we are also freed to enjoy his good gifts in their proper place. Compared to God himself, the controllers, the merit-earned blessings and the devil who lies behind the legalism, are a reduction of life's purpose, a religiously trivial pursuit.

Legalism always reduces life. The reduced life misses the point, which is to glorify God by serving, worshipping (two sides of the same coin), honouring, resting in, growing in, rejoicing in, learning from, loving and finding glad sufficiency in God himself. By such means, God is robbed by our legalism.

8

Old, Gnarled and Twisted

What do we become?

If this question isn't too late, what sort of a person do you want
to be when you're old? The question keeps cropping up for me
– young though I am (!) I watch other men age and I see that
even fine Christians, used by God and respected widely, can
become hard and irascible old men who habitually dismiss a
younger generation, deriding their lack of some key virtue
thought still to be possessed by the older generation. I see men
who have been innovators become entrenched and fixed. I see
men once known for their understanding and compassion
become intolerant and impatient. Sometimes you can discern
the simple wearing down of the soul by pain, or frustrating lim-
itations, disappointment or fear – or all four. Sometimes you
can discern the faults of youth coming home to roost.

What do we become? What does a legalist become?

The Krumholz condition

Trees that grow at high altitude, between the forest line and the
tree line (between where you can grow lots of trees and where

no trees will grow), tend to grow as distorted versions of lower-altitude specimens. They are often bent over, and are usually gnarled and twisted. It's a state called the Krumholz condition. Legalism distorts and misshapes us as we progress through life. Depriving us of the resources of God that are needed for healthy growth, it produces a kind of Christian Krumholz condition. The mindset of legalism has, I think, four ways of twisting us as we grow older; four ways of making us gnarled on the inside.

Despair

It creates quiet, background despair. Rules have a way of multiplying. Certainly if they are being used as pit-props to stop the roof caving in on our heavenly hope, they need to multiply. As we grow older we see fresh avenues of sin open up before us. The devil brings new sins to our attention and paints in disarmingly attractive colours rebellions that we had never dreamed we would find enticing. We need more and more rules to prevent us from novel transgressions. For most Christians the awareness of weakness heightens as the years pass.

The problem, the really self-destructive problem, is that you cannot keep all the rules. At the very time when your sense of sin and personal weakness grows, you are confronted with more broken rules. Brand new failures and disqualifications nag at you. This is more common than we bright young things might suspect. A Christian's sense of significance and worth can go down as the years add up. Grey hairs might crown an increasingly troubled mind. With sadistic cruelty, the enemy of our souls plagues us with accusation after accusation. He parades our deficiencies before our closing eyes, jabs at our hearts, robs us of peace and rest. Our self-esteem plummets and our assurance of the Father's love evaporates from under our feet. The quiet and hidden despair can break out in torrents of inconsolable woe. It happens.

It doesn't happen overnight, however: it happens through a lifelong attempt to deserve what God gives by grace through faith: an attempt marked by failure and an unremitting blocking out of the wonders of God's grace and power. Despite our best efforts – and in truth, because of *our* best efforts – we have never rested in God. By our best efforts we have constantly been running up a summit-less hill. We have never quite rested in the unconditional acceptance that becomes the ground from which we work. Our work has constantly been the ground from which we have tried to become accepted. Never has his grace been completely sufficient for all our needs. 'Such depths of forgiveness needed Lord – surely your grace can't reach that far down?' The nagging doubt has always disturbed the peace. 'What if I haven't done this or that well enough? What if this or that sin was repented of inadequately?' We reap what we, and others who failed to teach us grace and show us grace, have sown. A happy and ripe old age eludes us; we experience anguish and rottenness in our bones; we reap a harvest of worry about God. It happens.

Pride

Legalism can twist and turn us in the opposite way, though. Not despair but pride can harden the human heart as the years go by. You can keep some of the rules, and your ability plays upon the vestiges of your fallen self-sufficiency. If it happens early on in our Christian life – because from the word go we've been drinking in legalistic milk – then we will have developed proud bones. In our formative years in Christ, a disastrous disfigurement takes place. Criteria for acceptance, ways of handling the Scriptures, a perception of God, patterns of prayer, worship, service, submissiveness to false lords, a framework for what it means to be a Christian – all these and more are laid down in a matrix of self-justifying, works-based teaching and hinting. But what happens when, with that kind of disposition, reinforced in some people by a psychological pre-disposition to define life and esteem in terms of rules, we grow older and broadly speaking succeed in those terms? Simple: we grow proud. In that kind of world if you lay down laws which you can keep (and of course that's the trick!) you will be persuaded, against all the demands of modesty and sobriety, to become well-pleased with yourself.

There's nothing wrong in being pleased with yourself, of course: it's just a matter of where you see yourself as being. If you think basically in terms of being apart from Christ and doing this Christian life thing on your own, albeit for him, then you will become pleased merely with yourself. If, on the other hand, you see yourself as being in Christ, with him having done all on your behalf and you being accepted in him, then there is open to you the possibility of being pleased with yourself because fundamentally you are pleased with him, in whom you live and move and have your being. On this line, being pleased with yourself is a derived pleasure: derived from being utterly delighted with Christ who is your life. In this case there is no room for pride. In the former case there is room for only proud self-satisfaction.

It does happen a lot with men, though we don't have the monopoly on it by any means. At the risk of sounding sexist, it seems to be a pattern in churches at both ends of many a Christian spectrum, that men get prouder as they get older. We can become intractable, stubborn; harder in the heart and tenser, less relaxed about the face. We can be permanently assessing and less willing to listen, learn and change. We become less meek, rarely yielding, less tender with our wives.

It happens for all sorts of reasons, not least because in most of our churches it's men who hold power and who exercise control, who set the rules along lines which they can easily keep and who grow comfortable with the elevated status that it all brings. It goes to both the head and the heart. The condition worsens when you add the likelihood that such men may do fairly well at work, enjoying a level of seniority both there and in their families. The reading on the 'deep-seated pride' gauge begins to rise. Then when we develop, as we often do with passing birthdays, a growing suspicion of young people, of less successful people, of those who don't know what they're talking about and those who make mistakes, of those who are of a different temperament and so on, you begin to see the needle on the gauge rise even further.

This smug complacency can be well-hidden, buried deeply beneath the accretions of spiritual make-up; hidden especially to the sufferer. This only serves to protect the illness. This attitude is at its most deadly precisely when it is deep in the heart and unaddressed, for there it infects the soul. Why? Because there the attitude conditions the relationship with God. You do think that you can keep yourself in the Father's good books. All the evidence is there. You have been doing it for years! And why, when it infects the soul, is it so deadly? Because, here's irony for you, it has done exactly the same for you as it has done for the despairing soul. It has grounded your assurance on self's performance. Not properly proud of Christ and boasting in him, you have become improperly proud of self and you are basically boasting in yourself. In the realm of performance-related pay, you are on a fat income with bonuses and dividends and you don't mind the prestige that you assume you have acquired. But such pride is an undetected cancer. Whilst you think you're doing well, you are deeply diseased. Standing, you are always only a hair's breadth from falling; strong, you are weak. And you weaken others by modelling a life of works-based righteousness.

Judgementalism

This distortion leads to another: judgementalism. Blessed with the house rules, you have an effective and simple tool for assessing everyone else. Clearly, this is not the same as discernment, which we are called to develop. The ability to read people and situations well is part and parcel of the wisdom that years should bring. But how easy it is for us to drift from discernment to censure, from the position of the clear-sighted juror to the high and mighty judge. Indeed, we affirm our self-satisfaction as we do so: we are being more rigorously righteous for such role-changing. After all, we reason, the judge does more than the juror to stamp out misconduct.

But we could hardly be more wrong.

In the first place, when the discernment is made according to what are merely house rules, we import criteria which have more to do with taste, tradition and temperament, than with the holiness or the grace of God. We fall into the very trap that Paul sprang when he wrote about passing judgement on people according to what they eat: 'The man who eats everything must not look down on him who does not, and the man who does not eat everything must not condemn the man who does, for God has accepted him' (Rom. 14:3).

In the second place, we go flatly against Christ. He taught that it is right to use discernment and that it is wrong to extend that into passing judgement on people. In a passage loaded with paradox and satire, he exposes and corrects the legalism of the day.

> Do not judge, or you too will be judged. For in the same way as you judge others, you will be judged, and with the measure you use, it will be measured to you. Why do you look at the speck of sawdust in your brother's eye and pay no attention to the plank in your own eye? How can you say to your brother, 'Let me take the speck out of your eye,' when all the time there is a plank in your own eye? You hypocrite, first take the plank out of your own eye, and then you will see clearly to remove the speck from your brother's eye. Do not give dogs what is sacred; do not throw your pearls to pigs. If you do, they may trample them under their feet, and then turn and tear you to pieces (Mt. 7:1-6).

You have to be able to discern three things: your own true condition (in the imagery of the passage, whether or not you've got a plank in your eye); what sort of company you are in (you have to know a pig or a dog when you see one); and what's holy and precious to God (you have to recognise and value a pearl when you have one). But Jesus expressly condemns the attitude of the person who makes their discernment the basis for passing judgment. It's a brilliantly taught lesson, and it is vital in the fight against the deadliness of legalism. Over against the legalistic church magistrates, there is only one real judge. As the apostles testified: 'He commanded us to preach to the people and to testify that he [Jesus] is the one whom God appointed as judge of the living and the dead' (Acts 10:42). There is only one judge: Jesus Christ.

Legalism never produces gracious and expansive souls, growing richer in compassion and wisdom as the years go by. You'd never run to a legalist with your moral failure, breakdown, temptation, depression. Unless you're a masochist.

Hypocrisy

As the plank and speck lesson teaches, there's one other way in which the legalist's heart grows gnarled and twisted, for legalism encourages, even protects hypocrisy. The word is interesting. Our English word is a simple anglicised version of the Greek *hupokrites*. In the classical Greek of Aristotle and Plato, the hypocrite was the actor, someone who played a part on the stage. In the Greek theatre, with large crowds seated in amphitheatres and with those in back rows being some distance from the stage (this is before contact lenses and specs!) actors wore clothing that made them larger than life – particularly masks. They appeared to be more than they were in order to be recognised as the character that they were portraying. So the word became a metaphor for anyone who was a pretender.

How does legalism turn us into hypocrites? It provides masks for us to wear at church. We can wear the mask by keeping a sufficient number of the rules. We can put on the face of the instantly recognisable 'good' Christian, while underneath we're an entirely different person. The right smile, the hands or hand going up on cue, or staying grimly in the pocket. The Bible on show. The dress code adhered to. Whatever. You know the details. As long as you keep up the appearances, defined as they are by the rules and regulations, you can be a cruel husband, a tyrannical mother, a lousy employee, a pervert, the list goes on. Or you can just be unforgiving, hard-hearted, bitter, jealous, spiteful, a sanctified offence-taker. As long as you smile the right way, have the right appearance and turn up at the right things – you're fine, in your own estimation.

Beautiful, but all too rare, is the fellowship where the really important things are gauged as honestly and perceptively as the obvious, visible and 'showy' things. Beautiful but rare is 'quick-eyed love'.

Worse: since legalism is essentially a *Godward* problem, the hypocrisy has a deeper and more pernicious dimension: we act with God. We needn't, of course. He sees through it all and is vastly unimpressed by the attempt. He knows all that there is to know, forgives our sins, accepts us in Christ, and is resolved to present us perfect before his throne at the last. But it is one of the weaknesses of the legalist mind-set that it thinks that we must come to God strong and that we define strength; that we must come to him not needing help and that we define the limits of helplessness. Who needs a great high priest who is able to sympathise with us in all our weaknesses, when with a few adept strokes of acting we can make ourselves look strong? Who needs a Proper Man when we can do propriety well enough ourselves, thank you very much? The mask-wearing stops us from coming to God in dependence upon him. Worse still, it prevents us from ever really dealing with the things that the mask hides. We do not open up to him and allow him to deal with the bruised and painful, or the dark and dying corners of our souls. Do legalists feel loved in their brokenness? Are they ever healed from the inner, hidden, crippling injuries of sin? Tragically, they are not. Does the soul of the legalist ever fully bask in the sunshine of God's grace?

Our contemporary versions of age-old legalism produce no great trees by the river, but only the stunted and twisted versions on the bare, cold heights. Krumholz Christians. God is robbed again. He is robbed of the glory that comes from a life which is increasingly filled with grace and faith. He is robbed by what the legalist's life becomes.

10

... But God is the Glorious Lord

There are two particular ways in which we can be freed from the legalism that robs God of his glory. The first has to do with the one who is Lord, and the second with living for the one who is also glorious.

Lord of the Conscience

Those aspects of legalism that rob him have a common thread running through them. They all involve the elevation of people in our churches to the position of what we might call 'lords-of-the-conscience'. They (we!) might do it themselves, but there's always a degree of complicity from others. The rest accept, to some degree, the false lordship that they exercise. We play along with the game of self-justification and self-created holiness, even if we do it against our better judgement.

The antidote to this is the Lordship of Christ.

'What? Isn't that just authoritarianism writ large: rules and regulations and do this and bossing about and style being cramped. Where does Lordship leave my individuality?'

It certainly seems to be a contradiction in terms to say that we can find a cure for the oppression of legalism in the absolute authority of another. At least, it seems like a contradiction if there's still a residue of the old fleshly antinomianism in us. If we're still longing for self-rule and still see freedom as being freedom to do whatever our hearts desire, then the idea of anyone lording it over us is bound to sound like a deepening of the problem.

But don't panic! We aren't consigned to an endless turmoil of irresolvable conflict between the lording of the legalists and our desire to call our own shots. For God is our Lord, who sets us free from the captivity to law and the captivity to sin.

Consider these medicinal words, balm to the oppressed soul, from the Westminster Confession of Faith:

> God alone is Lord of the conscience, and hath left it free from the doctrines and commandments of men, which are, in anything, contrary to His Word, or beside it (that is, placed on the same level as the Word), in matters of faith or worship. So that to believe such doctrines, or to obey such commands out of conscience, is to betray true liberty of conscience: and the requiring of an implicit faith, and an absolute and blind obedience, is to destroy liberty of conscience, and reason also (chapter 20:2).

Granted, the Westminster Confession hasn't made it to the Top Ten Christian Book list for a while (the cover's grotty for one thing!) and it's unlikely to be voted as the next Christian Book of the Year. The paragraph above might even be a little off-putting, being in the old tongue and all that. That said, the biblical teaching that the passage expresses really is balm for bruised souls. It collates a range of biblical passages and a way of thinking which, though set against the Catholicism of the day, are still of the most immensely therapeutic value.

So much so, that the words are still read out as part of the service of the induction of a new minister in the Presbyterian Church in Ireland. A few weeks ago I was sitting in a church on the infamous Shankhill Road in Belfast as a good friend was becoming its next minister. I knew that the passage from the

Westminster Confession was coming, but it still was arresting to
hear the words ringing out. They sounded a warning to the congregation and to Noel, the new minister: 'Don't any of you get
above yourselves now!' They also sounded the most eloquent
reprieve from the relentless onslaught of religious traditions

No infallible pastors!

The passage from the Westminster Confession says: You need
never again suffer under anyone, but anyone, who assumes the
authority of Christ in your life. Christ alone is lord of your conscience. (No, for the knee-jerkingly anti-antinomian among us,
it does not, repeat not, say that you can do what you like. It does
not give anyone permission to become a loose cannon firing off
volleys of sin on a whim. It does teach that you've a conscience
and that your conscience is expected to function under the
lordship of Christ.)

   Your pastor might claim to be infallible (as some do, explicitly or more dangerously, implicitly); your group leader might
claim that they speak as God's appointed prophet so if you don't
do what they say, some kind of (wait for it folks) 'Ananias and
Sapphira anointing' will fall on you. (*Don't* laugh: this gets said
and tragically it gets believed.) Your church might place such
emphasis on the exposition of the Scriptures by the teaching
elder that he (and it probably would be a he) acquires and
enjoys the kind of power that a seventeenth century Pope
would have envied. Despite all claims to the contrary no-one,
but *no-one* has the place of Christ over your conscience. These
others are only blokes. As the saying goes, they put their trousers
on the same way as you do (even if you're a girl!)

No other master

'God alone is Lord of the conscience.' Where does that come
from? It comes from two passages. James 4:12: 'There is only

one Lawgiver and Judge, the one who is able to save and destroy. But you, who are you to judge your neighbour?' And Romans 14:2-4:

> One man's faith allows him to eat everything (No, not in the sense of gluttony!), but another man, whose faith is weak, eats only vegetables. The man who eats everything must not look down on him who does not, and the man who does not eat everything must not condemn the man who does, for God has accepted him. Who are you to judge someone else's servant? To his own master he stands or falls. And he will stand, for the Lord is able to make him stand.

Why is no-one else to be Christ to your conscience? Because no-one else could or has purchased you at great price from your captivity to sin and the law; no-one has the right to wrest you from his liberating service and press you into theirs, as if you were their servant. Especially not Satan.

Your conscience, then, is 'free from the doctrines and commandments of men, which are, in anything, contrary to His Word, or beside it (that is, placed on the same level as the Word), in matters of faith or worship.' If anyone teaches anything that either contradicts God's word or claims to be on the same level as it, they are wrong, and you don't have to do what they say. Where did the theologians at Westminster get that teaching? They got it from examples and statements in Scripture that show just how clearly the early church had grasped that Christ had sole rights to their complete obedience. For instance, we have the example of Peter and John before the rulers, elders and teachers of the law in Jerusalem (Acts 4:5-6).

Just to remind us of who Peter had once been so afraid of, Luke points out that Annas the high priest was there, and so were Caiaphas, John, Alexander and the other men of the high priest's family. This is the very grouping that had tried Jesus; in their stronghold Peter had been so fearful that his love for Christ was driven out and replaced by vehement denials. But now Peter is under the control of a different Spirit. No longer self-strengthened and therefore weak, he is filled with the Spirit of God and so is truly strong. So when the powerful and deeply religious commanders of the conscience tell the apostles not to go around speaking in the name of Jesus, that is, in the authority and under the will of Jesus, Peter and John parry their law-giving blow and then riposte with those courageous and unanswerable words 'Judge for yourselves whether it is right in God's sight to obey you rather than God' (v.19). It is a straight contest between two Lords of the conscience. Jesus wins!

We also have the commendation of the Bereans in Acts 17:11: 'Now the Bereans were of more noble character than the Thessalonians, for they received the message with great eagerness and examined the Scriptures every day to see if what Paul said was true.' Anyone else's say-so had only a conditional hold upon the believers – conditional upon it being under the authority of the Word of God. And we have Paul giving an account of his clash with legalism in the whole of Galatians 2.

The Westminster divines also got this teaching from the gospels, in which Jesus freed his disciples not only from the pretended lordship of the enemies of the gospel, but also from each other, lest any of them get ideas above their station! Matthew 23:8-10 says: 'But you are not to be called "Rabbi", for you have only one Master and you are all brothers. And do not call anyone on earth "father", for you have one Father, and he is in heaven. Nor are you to be called "teacher", for you have one Teacher, the Christ.' In case there's a residue of doubt about whose word to listen to, God's or man's, see what Jesus said in conflict with the legalists who took such determined dispute with him: 'He replied, "Isaiah was right when he prophesied about you hypocrites; as it is written: 'These people honour me with their lips, but their hearts are far from me. They worship me in vain; their teachings are but rules taught by men.' You have let go of the commands of God and are holding on to the traditions of men"' (Mk 7:6-8).

Don't yield to earthly gods

Moreover, to teach us that we have a responsibility before God to refuse to yield to these earthly powers, we are reminded of those Scriptures which teach that 'to believe such doctrines, or to obey such commands out of conscience, is to betray true liberty of conscience.' Hear the echo of Colossians 2:20-23

> Since you died with Christ to the basic principles of this world, why, as though you still belonged to it, do you submit to its rules: 'Do not handle! Do not taste! Do not touch!'? These are all destined to perish with use, because they are based on human commands and teachings. Such regulations indeed have an appearance of wisdom, with their self-imposed worship, their false humility and their harsh treatment of the body, but they lack any value in restraining sensual indulgence.

Hear the echo of Paul's testimony of how he and his companions had reacted to the legalistic Judaizers: 'This matter arose because some false brothers had infiltrated our ranks to spy on the freedom we have in Christ Jesus and to make us slaves. We did not give in to them for a moment, so that the truth of the gospel might remain with you' (Gal 2:4-5).

Don't lose the head

To make the sinfulness of legalism even clearer, these supposedly hard-hearted and unyielding puritans also wrote that 'the requiring of an implicit faith, and an absolute and blind obedience, is to destroy liberty of conscience, and reason also.' They picked up on the kind of thing that the Old Testament prophets said. This is from Jeremiah 8:8-9: 'How can you say,

"We are wise, for we have the law of the LORD", when actually the lying pen of the scribes has handled it falsely? The wise will be put to shame; they will be dismayed and trapped. Since they have rejected the word of the LORD, what kind of wisdom do they have?' This is God's word through Isaiah to those who would teach the children of God to consult mediums and spirits: 'To the law and to the testimony! If they do not speak according to this word, they have no light of dawn' (Is. 8:20). And lest we are in any doubt, this is from Jesus, who lived what he spoke:

> Jesus called them together and said, 'You know that the rulers of the Gentiles lord it over them, and their high officials exercise authority over them. Not so with you. Instead, whoever wants to become great among you must be your servant, and whoever wants to be first must be your slave – just as the Son of Man did not come to be served, but to serve, and to give his life as a ransom for many' (Mt.20:25-28).

Christ's Lordship means our freedom

What am I saying by referring to the Westminster Confession? I'm saying that to bind the conscience to Christ the Lord is in fact to liberate it from the tyrannies of fallen man and of the devil. The legalism that the authors of the Confession faced might not be the version that many of the readers of this book have suffered under. It might not even have been the one around in the days of the New Testament. But the principles that we read in the Confession were derived from the Bible and apply to us. In that biblical teaching lies the corrective for those who would run from legalism into antinomianism. In that same teaching lies the reproach to those who would label as sinful or rebellious anyone who rejects their legalistic control. And in that teaching lies the route to a life that no longer robs God of obedience to his sole lordship.

The need for gracious brass neck!

This is not an easy cure to apply. Legalism works best upon those in our fellowships who are youngest in the faith and/or those who feel a strong need for the acceptance and approval of those leaders to whom they look up. It takes a measure of inner conviction, biblical understanding and plain brass neck to refuse to knuckle under and conform. But it also takes a measure of grace and spiritual maturity to be able to do this in love, rather than in a merely selfish strop. Struggling out from under the burden of legalism is not about self-assertiveness so much as about asserting the Lordship of Christ in your life. It is humility before God that gives a Christian courage before the traditions of men and, sometimes, the men of tradition. Fearing God, we learn to fear no-one else.

The wonderful thing is that you can have a mind that really reckons on the Lordship of Christ, that is truly controlled by the Spirit and that is being renewed by the word of God. You can gain from his active word the clarity of insight, the strength of character and the wisdom to know both when and how to be your new self. And you can thereby be your proper self before God without becoming merely selfish.

Resilience against being judged by another's conscience comes easily to some but not so easily to others. The refusal to be swayed by what others might say – and they will say! – can be psychologically difficult to muster, especially if you're genuinely afraid of simply being thoughtless or unloving. Paul, who wrote 'why should my freedom be judged by another's conscience?' went on to write 'Do not cause anyone to stumble, whether Jews, Greeks or the church of God' (1Cor. 10:23ff). It might be difficult to achieve a blend of unselfish love, thoughtfulness towards the legalist, submission to the liberating lordship of Christ and assertiveness of his lordship over against any other lord. But God can give us just such a blend of characteristics. Consider the coalescence of terms that James works with when he writes: 'Scripture says: "God opposes the proud but gives grace to the humble." Submit yourselves, then, to God. Resist the devil, and he will flee from you' (Jas. 4:6-7). The bad words – proud, devil – stand in stark contrast to those whom God blesses with his grace – the humble, those submissive to God, who resist the devil, who see the devil flee.

It is that same nuanced Christian personality that Peter writes about when he advises young men (who can certainly suffer under the oppressive power of legalism and tragically, can emulate it) to be submissive to those who are older. 'All of you, clothe yourselves with humility towards one another, because, "God opposes the proud but gives grace to the humble." Humble yourselves, therefore, under God's mighty hand, that he may lift you up in due time' (1Pet. 5:5,6).

We need courage for this cure to work. God has bound you to himself. He is the only Lord of heaven and earth: he alone is the one with the final authority. The one who is eternally for you is the one who sets you free from the burden of legalism. He cures us by his sweeping, awesome sovereignty, the infinitely imperious grace of his lordship. God gives courage; he gives himself and he is under no-one's thumb!

Give Him the glory

The final cure for legalism is the briefest to describe, yet the best. Live for the glory of God.

He is worthy of all the glory

God's great goal is his glory. That can sound egocentric to us, can't it? It is egocentric for us to have our own glory as our great goal in life, but then we are not God. For him it's exactly right. He made all that he has made for himself – for his pleasure. No one was forcing him to make any of it: he made all things by his own free and sovereign will and he did so in his grace. He is worthy of all the glory because he made us. No one was forcing him to redeem those who strayed from him. For his pleasure – just because he wanted to in his great mercy – he sent his one and only Son to bring us back to himself. He is worthy of all the glory that we can give him because he has redeemed us.

The heavens declare the glory of God. So can we, who have strayed so far and yet who have been brought back at such cost to him. He rightly will not share his glory with another: he will not have us place anyone or anything else alongside him as a rival for our worship and love. He is glorified in our exclusive worship of him and love for him. He is glorified as we find our joy in him, our sufficient strength and peace in him, our guidance, our values, our light, our hope, our pleasures, our satisfaction in him.

Luther wrote about the life of faith being the out-turned life. The legalistic life of works is turned in upon itself in self-examination, self-doubt, self-castigation, self-satisfaction. But the life of faith, by which we depend upon the grace of God and submit to the Lordship of Christ alone gives us a new focus: God himself. We are turned outward, upward, Godward.

Many things happen in this process, but one of them is especially liberating from the clutches of legalism. The more that his glory is your goal and delight, the more you will learn to spot those false spiritualities which ultimately glorify men and women. You will more quickly recognise power- or control-hungry Christians and fellowships; and you will spot the same hungers within yourself. Increasing Christ-likeness means that we increasingly live for the glory of God, as he did and does. He lived, died, and lived again in order to glorify his Father. He even gives the glory that he receives from the Father back to the Father: one day he will be confessed and yielded to as Lord to the glory of the Father. As we become like him in this God-glorifying way, that which is less than God will neither satisfy us nor master us.

Prepare for glory

There is nothing like the forward-looking and upwardly-mobile life (a life moving heavenward) to make the legalism of church life clearly apparent and transparently false. It's not real holiness; it never produces the largeness of heart that Christ produces; it gives no delight and satisfaction to the soul; it gives no glory to God. It is so obviously *not* what you were made for and no-one would have died to save you into that. It is not what you're destined for either. The day will come when this often rebellious heart, that still finds it so hard to bow before God, will be in glory and there will bow. These resurrected knees will bend. This resurrected tongue will cry 'You are worthy, our Lord and God, to receive glory and honour and power, for you created all things, and by your will they were created and have their being' (Rev. 4:11). From our risen souls will flood praise and honour to the Lamb who was slain. Our lips shall be among those that will sing the song of Revelation 5:13: 'To him who sits on the throne and to the Lamb be praise and honour and glory and power, for ever and ever!'

The day will come when we shall cry out with a loud voice: 'Salvation belongs to our God, who sits on the throne, and to the Lamb' (Rev. 7:10). At our final destination no one will steal glory from God, no one will claim credit for their own salvation, only Jesus will be called Lord. Over against the tyrannies of the flesh and the counter-demands of pathetic false gods this shout that we read in Revelation shall ring out louder than thunder and we shall be shouting it with the great multitude in heaven: 'Hallelujah! Salvation and glory and power belong to our God, for true and just are his judgments … Hallelujah! For our Lord God Almighty reigns. Let us rejoice and be glad and give him glory!'

That's where you and I are going. Why prepare for anything less? Live for the glory of God. Therein lies your point and purpose in life; therein lies your own true glory. In living by faith alone in the grace of God alone and for the glory of God alone lies your true freedom from the corrupting sin of legalism. In such freedom you will find heaven begun on earth.